THE CHRISTIAN AND HIS AMERICA

HARPER & BROTHERS PUBLISHERS

NEW YORK

HARPER & BROTHERS PUBLISHERS

NEW YORK

THE

CHRISTIAN

AND

HIS

AMERICA

BY GERALD KENNEDY

Library of Congress catalog card number: 56-12068

THIS IS FOR MY BROTHER

Contents

Contents

Preface

No one really sees America until he has looked at it from the outside, and then traveled through its rich and varied land. My work during the last eight years has given me both of these experiences, which has resulted in a certain basic conviction. I believe that America is a faith and its greatness is rooted in Christianity. Let us not argue over the extent to which the Founding Fathers were orthodox Christians. Their whole political philosophy is immersed in the teachings of Jesus Christ and their basic assumptions rest on the Biblical interpretation of human nature. Christians must play an ever-increasing role in the contemporary American scene, and the Christian Church is the decisive factor in determining the American destiny. Our moral and spiritual blind spots can be illuminated only by individual citizens committing themselves to the Christian gospel.

The first part analyzes the delusions of democracy. The second part describes the functions of the Christian's high calling in a society like ours. The third part interprets the demands which God puts upon Christians in times like these.

The book is an expansion of the Ayer Lectures delivered at Colgate-Rochester Divinity School in the spring of 1955. This lectureship was founded in 1928 by Mr. and Mrs. Wildred W. Fry in memory of Mrs. Fry's father, the late Francis Wayland Ayer. My thanks go to President Wilbour E. Saunders and other friends at the Seminary who made my visit such a pleasure and joy.

Thanks to my wife who not only listened to all of this when first delivered but came in with the right responses at the right time and then read every word. Without her criticisms this would be worse than it is.

Hollywood, California   GERALD KENNEDY

I

DELUSIONS

I

The Myth of Superman

EDMUND BURKE HAS BEEN CLAIMED BY BOTH CONSERVATIVES AND liberals, which means probably that he had a mind of such depth and breadth that it is not possible to confine him within artificial boundaries. The great man belongs to all men. In a speech delivered in Buckinghamshire in 1784, he made a far-reaching observation about freedom and human nature. Said he, "The people never give up their liberties but under some delusion." That will be the secular text of what I want to discuss in these three chapters.

At the risk of oversimplification, it may be asserted that all philosophies fall into one of two main categories. Either they believe that salvation is of God or they believe it is of man. Church members may believe the latter, and skeptics may believe the former. We can be fooled by words and phrases, but the truth about a man's way of life is revealed when he is driven to the wall and he turns toward the object of his final confidence. Then there is discovered an inarticulate faith, or sometimes a hidden atheism. The time of crisis has a way of stripping off the veneer of our pretenses and revealing our means of support, or lack of it.

In our century, we have been shocked by the behavior of so-called civilized peoples. We discovered that even the pious words of faith had lost their meanings and the inner rooms of the soul were bare. We discovered the old gods were not dead, but sleeping, and that the long Christian centuries had not destroyed the idols. Suddenly, or at least so it seemed, men reverted to the worship of a kind of superman, who was actually a kind of subman. Force, ruthlessness, cruelty, and the ability to instill fear were his claims to authority.

Once again it became apparent that William Penn was right when he said that man would either obey God or the Tyrant.

It would not be so bad if this were confined to isolated places. But it is in the air, here in the New World as well as abroad. We Americans have had to face in our generation, as did our fathers before us, the delusion that salvation is from some superman. The Christian Church is the main protector against such madness, and as Christians we have a terrifying responsibility to ourselves and to the world. To this superman delusion we must turn our attention.

I.   DISAPPOINTMENTS OF DEMOCRACY

Too many people assume that democracy is all promise and no demand. When India became an independent nation, many Indian citizens assumed that all their troubles were over. They were to obtain their desires without price and they were to travel on the trains without fares. When it does not turn out this way, many people are disillusioned and feel that democracy has betrayed them. The truth is that democracy as a way of life is difficult and demanding. It demands faith and confidence in unseen and unprovable propositions. It is never too difficult to find weaknesses and inconsistencies in it, so that one may have a field day in describing its foibles.

For one thing, a democracy is wide open to the power of emotional appeals, and it can easily become the victim of waves of hysteria. One of the main arguments for an authoritarian church or for a state church is the rampant emotionalism characterizing the uncontrollable sects and cults. When one listens to some of the Sunday fare served up on the American radio, one wonders if this freedom is not doing more harm than good. If this is the only religion vast numbers of Americans are familiar with, it is not surprising that our religious life is so often sentimental, obscurantist, and irrelevant.

But religion is not the only thing to be cheapened and sold to the masses. Economics makes a good product to adulterate, package at-

tractively, and peddle to the people who still have not learned that
two and two are four. Times of turmoil have seen the blossoming
of hotbed schemes which offer easy money and financial panaceas.
There is no guarantee that some scheme might not one day obtain
a majority at the polls and wreck the economy of the state. This can
be extremely risky business.

Or, there is politics, which is a natural for emotionalism and sales-
manship. We have been living in a time when honorable men have
been pursued, and in a few instances caught, by second-rate politicians without ethics but with persuasive tongues. A hero-hungry,
frustrated, and uncertain people might be stampeded by a man rid-
ing in on a horse, or be seduced by a clever, self-designated savior.
It is no wonder that conservative minds have been suspicious of
democracy and quick to point out the perils of such a way. The
long view of American democracy, however, gives us courage for
the future. We have had our uneasy moments, especially after our
wars, but the recuperative and recreative capacity of our democratic
tradition has always shown the vitality to reconstruct and to rebuild
on solid foundations. The good sense and judgment of the people
have time and again reasserted themselves and we have recovered
our realism and sanity. The democratic process has vindicated
itself and, when compared with other ways, it seems to be amply
worthy of our faith.

For example, look at the General Conference of the Methodist
Church. I use this because I am more familiar with it, though the
governing assembly of any of our churches would serve as well.
This quadrennial conference makes most of the final decisions for
my church and it passes the legislation. It has been under considerable emotional pressure from time to time, and small powerful
groups have endeavored to promote special, emergency action.
Seldom has the General Conference yielded. One has an increased
respect for this body, as one considers its history in the light of
what might have been. A cross section of the ministers and laymen

of the Methodist Church are hard to stampede, and they exhibit a reassuring sense of Christian justice and propriety. The same thing can be said for the American Republic and for the British Commonwealth.

Again, democracy seems notoriously inefficient. The longer processes of debate and vote seem hopelessly involved and cumbersome to many people. You will recall that one of the main reasons for some Americans' early enthusiasm for Mussolini was that he made the trains run on time. One of my friends, after a frustrating experience with a church committee, said that, if the children of Israel had depended on committees, they would still be in Egypt. Ah, yes! Congressional debates are not always on a dignified plane, nor are they always relevant to the issues involved. Sometimes our government representatives appear to be the descendants of Nero, and fiddle while the world burns. It can hardly be denied that there is much overlapping and waste among government agencies, yet there is a curious reluctance to follow the recommendations of a Hoover Committee or anyone else bent on economy and efficiency.

Elmer Davis is of the opinion that the whole structure of our government aims to prevent too much efficiency. It was set up with checks and balances so that it would not move too swiftly. The Founding Fathers preferred time for debate and consideration, that the people might have an opportunity to hear the issues discussed and then to express themselves. If efficiency had been the ultimate goal, then the Constitution would have been set in a different frame.

Yet again we must say that the record is good. We have managed to fight wars, go through depressions, and assume world leadership. No one will deny that there have been some rather dangerous moments, nor can we escape the fact that our modern situation allows less time for decision. But in the day of crisis we have been able to give authority to our leaders and accept their commands with what grace we could muster. And we have been able to restore the final authority to the people when the emergency was past.

But no one will insist that we have always chosen the safest way. Freedom is expensive and it is dangerous. We are so hard to teach, and we forget so soon. We are not yet out of the woods. As a matter of fact, we never will be.

2. SUPERMAN'S APPEAL

One of the early stories of Israel concerns the decision to have a king "like all the nations." "But the thing displeased Samuel." Yet they had their king, though it was no real answer to their problems.

There is in men a desire for authority, or perhaps it is better to say there is a necessity for authority. There has to be some kind of order to live by and some final loyalty for human nature. The sense of drifting can be endured for only a short time, and then comes a submission to whatever leader is available. Life is a quest for a legitimate object of loyalty, and disaster occurs when men have yielded their allegiance to the cause or man which betrays them. The basic problem is freedom, for it can so easily be mistaken for license, which in turn tempts us to deny authority altogether.

Protestants are supposed to believe in a free church in contrast to the authoritarian viewpoint of their Catholic brethren. The contrast is not so marked as it is sometimes described. I have been face to face with authoritarian lust on the part of laymen and preachers in Protestant churches which would yield nothing to the Roman Catholic hierarchy. A layman once wrote to me and gave directions for the solution of the problem in his church. He even promised to pray that I would be led to do God's will. When the Cabinet's idea of God's will did not coincide with his, I received another letter complaining that the Methodist Church no longer had any authority in its government.

There are men who in the same pronouncement will insist that the bishop must speak for no one but himself, and then criticize him because he does not fire a dozen preachers and silence a score of laymen. We want authority, if it will do what we want it to do and quiet all the dissenting voices. The idea of a superman, who will brook no nonsense and will crack the whip, has a big appeal to many men if they can be sure that such a fellow will see things as they see them. There are not many who are willing to risk their ideas in the open competition of the market.

On a bicycle trip through Germany in 1935 I met a man in the inn of a small town near Berlin. He was a Nazi and spoke glowingly of what Hitler was doing for Germany. I have not forgotten the look of relief on his face as he said, "Whatever he commands, I will do." Back of that confession was a long period of unemployment, frustration, fear, defeat. He was tired of living without faith and assurance, so that finding a man who would take the responsibility for the decisions was what he wanted most of all.

Responsibility is a heavy burden to bear, and the man without spiritual resources can hardly carry it. That best-selling novel *From Here to Eternity* illustrated it. Many men in the peacetime army were bitter and critical, and they counted the days until their enlistment was ended and they could be free men again. But when the time came and they wandered about rootless for a time, it suddenly dawned on them that they must now provide for themselves so much which they had accepted from the army without thought. They would have to find a job, a place to live, buy clothes and food, and make a hundred new decisions. As a result, most of them went back and re-enlisted, for they had been out of civilian life too long.

After the war, a number of my young men came back from military service and shared with their pastor their new problems. Often there was no housing for them and they moved in with their wives' families, which was not easy for any of those concerned. Their jobs were not very interesting, and the welcome back was not nearly so cordial as they had anticipated. Living costs were high and there were financial problems. They had dreamed of getting home, they often confessed, but they had not imagined anything except daily rejoicings. But now they were remembering that military life was not so bad. The burden of civilian responsibilities was heavier than they could carry.

Fascism exerts its appeal to those who are weary of labor relations, unemployment, and competition. It promises security from change and social upheaval. Communism gives an answer to all the questions of destiny, and substitutes commands for the necessity of choice. We have made too little of this part of the totalitarian appeal. It is not always a conversion to a new economic or social theory, but simply a vast weariness that brings converts into the fold. Our danger is not of rivals with greater appeal. We must fear a faithless generation seeking something to fill its emptiness, even if it be nothing more than glowing, empty promises.

In 1831, Disraeli, traveling in Egypt, met Mehemet Ali, a rascal who had made himself master of the country. He was toying with the idea of establishing a parliamentary form of government, and asked Disraeli for his comments. The British statesman took a dim view of the idea and pointed out a number of difficulties in the way. But at the next meeting the Pasha beamed as he gave his solution to the problem. "God is great!" he began. "You are a wise man. Allah! Kerim, but you spit pearls. Nevertheless, I will have a parliament, and I will have as many parliaments as the King of England himself. See here!" He flourished two lists of names. "Here are my parliaments; but I have made up my mind, to prevent inconvenience, to elect them myself."[1] Many a man wishes he might escape the inconveniences of democracy by some superman tactic.

3. SUPERMEN FAIL

One theme that runs through all of the Bible is that trust in men offers no sound basis for security. "It is better to take refuge in

the Lord," says Psalm 118:9 "than to put confidence in princes."
Israel never learned the lesson completely, and neither have we.
But if history could teach us anything beyond dispute, it is that
supermen are weak reeds to lean on.

No man is wise enough to play the part of superman. Anyone
put in a position where he must make important decisions soon
learns that the checks and balances of many minds are his only
safety. A man presents a specific situation as he sees it. There may
be no question concerning his honesty and sincerity. But no individual is ever able to see the whole scene, and it is always necessary
to wait for other views. The art of government is not dependent
ultimately on absolute consistency, but it is dependent on wise
compromise and much patience. To move swiftly and ruthlessly
forward in pursuit of a policy may be the road to immediate accomplishment, but not necessarily to solid achievement. A broad base
is a necessity when it comes to guiding people.

Any city must listen to much testimony before the council dares
to decide even relatively unimportant matters. For the effects of a
policy can never be visualized entirely, and what seems to be a
good idea can wreak havoc on some easily ignored groups. In this
department, experts are never enough, for the decision is a human
one and not always technical.

One of my friends was elevated to a position very near the top
of his profession. One member of his family was playing an important role in federal government, and he was in the habit of
moving among people whose names were household words in
America. He sat with me one evening and talked about famous
people he knew. "The most disillusioning thing about them," he
said, "is to discover that they are not much smarter than I am."
He went on to say that people assume that such leaders must be
superior persons in every way, having wisdom far above the ordinary man. Actually, they are men with prejudices and selfishnesses
and flaws in their thinking, the same as the man next door. God

has not bestowed on a few leaders enough wisdom to make the decisions for a society.

But even more serious than lack of wisdom is lack of goodness. No man is good enough to wield unlimited power. Corruption is universal, and no class of men is immune from it. A popular theory says that men of wealth are the culprits, and if they can be limited in their influence, society will be democratic. One can hardly deny that the nineteenth-century "robber barons" often rode roughshod over the rights of the public. Their exploitation of our natural resources for immediate profit was not a pretty picture, and it is not to be wondered that there was a terrific reaction.

Today labor has more power than was dreamed of one hundred years ago. This has certainly helped to restore the balance. But would anyone contend that the champions of labor are always incorruptible when they are wielding tremendous power? The record does not so indicate, and we are driven to the conclusion that, without checks, the public will suffer exploitation from this source.

Then someone comes along and says that Big Government must be umpire between Big Business and Big Labor. But behold! another danger. Because a man works for the government is no guarantee that he cannot be contaminated by the lust for power. An overgrown bureaucracy invades the fields of freedom, as the jungle invades cultivated land. It can become the enemy of responsibility and betray the idea of service to the community. Man is man, whether his chief interests lie in one field or another, and the idea that we can solve our problems by substituting one class for another is a part of the sentimental nonsense of communism. Even the Church provides no automatic protection, and one of the unloveliest sights in the world is a churchman corrupted by his pride of power and trying in vain to make it more palatable by a covering of piosity.

Bernard Shaw wrote:

A critic recently described me as having "a kindly dislike of my fellow creatures." Dread would have been nearer the mark than dislike; for man is the only animal of which I am thoroughly and cravenly afraid. I have never thought much of the courage of a lion tamer. Inside the cage he is at least safe from other men. There is less harm in a well-fed lion. It has no ideals, no sect, nor party, no nation, no class: in short, no reason for destroying anything it does not want to eat.[2]

And when one sees what men can do under the delusion of power, these sentiments appear entirely reasonable.

When a man seeks to become more than a man he becomes less than a man. The whole concept of some superhuman leadership being discovered or trained by society is doomed to failure, even when set forth eloquently by a Plato. When Albert Schweitzer received the Nobel Peace Prize, he said, "But the essential fact which must now strike home to us (and it should have struck home long ago) is that inhumanity and the superman are indissolubly linked; the one progresses in step with the other."

The depth of Christian understanding is revealed in its doctrine of man. Chesterton pointed out that Christianity separated the two viewpoints of man, exaggerated both of them, and then held them together in a creative tension. In so far as I am Man I am a little lower than the angels and the chief of creatures. But as a man I am a sinner standing in the need of redemption. We are not to yield to the pessimism that makes a man less than the brutes, nor are we to echo Homer's despair, that we are the saddest of all the beasts of the field. We are the creatures of God, made in his image, full of glory and majesty, yet doomed to madness and destruction when we lose our humility.

No man dares to seek release from the commonplace. A diplomat was shocked to find President Lincoln shining his shoes. "Do you polish your own shoes?" he exclaimed, "Yes," Lincoln answered, "whose shoes do you polish?" I do not know anything except the Christian faith which will keep man's attitude toward himself accurate and honest.

4. GOD AND LEADERS

Leadership is a matter of service and, as the ancient collect says, only in the service of God do we find our freedom. A leadership based on position, rank, power, or privilege is a betrayal of society and leads to its destruction. When we can no longer produce leadership that seeks to serve, our way is at an end and our faith is dead. It must be obvious that this is a religious affair, for without spiritual undergirding we shall become dictator ridden or the tyrant's victims.

Christianity does not depend on democracy, but democracy depends on Christianity, and in no place is it more clearly illustrated than in the quality of leadership demanded by a democracy. When we see the contrast between a Führer or a Duce and an American President, we are aware of two separate worlds of thought and two opposed philosophies of leadership. Our roots go back to the Bible, and especially to the New Testament. The difference is summed up in our Lord's rebuke of his Disciples, when they strove for the first places in the coming Kingdom. As Jesus led them through Galilee, teaching them of the coming tragedy of the Cross, they came at evening to Capernaum. "What were you discussing on the way?" he asked them. They had not realized he had overheard them and they were ashamed to tell him, for they had been arguing about who was the greatest. It would be enlightening to learn the reasons each man gave for his superiority over the others. Then Jesus laid down one of the fundamental principles of his teaching: "If any one would be first, he must be last of all and servant of all" (Mark 9:34).*

The Church may forget and ignore this standard of leadership, but, more than any other organization, the Church is the embodiment and manifestation of this idea. Christian leaders have so often

* Unless otherwise noted Biblical references are to *The Holy Bible, Revised Standard Version*, Nelson, 1952.

come from the humble classes that this fact is sometimes used as a reproach. But this is one of the chief glories of the Church, for its leadership is not bound by the artificial rules of class or status. It means that the greatest are the servants.

To the extent that the democratic ideal guides us, this must also be true for the nation. The further we get from the possibility of any poor boy becoming the President of the United States, the closer we approach the aristocratic ideal of society. The superman philosophy assumes that such creatures are the reason for a society to exist, but Christianity insists that leaders exist to serve their fellows. There are people who still repeat the words of service, but they have no belief that they are true, and the rootless words die and all they stood for fades. Only if men are the servants of God, whose service is best expressed through service to men, can this democratic doctrine of leadership be maintained.

Each man must play his part if our society is to have stability. A few supermen, leading masses of despised peasants, lack the power to endure. The base must be broad, and each person must be aware of his dignity and responsibility. The age of faith produces men by the score who eagerly await an opportunity to play their part, while the age of doubt cries out in vain for leaders. It is not true that only a few men are endowed with the gifts of wisdom and devotion, for the plain man, when made aware of his divine status, often proves to have insights, courage, and a good sense of direction.

But we shall not argue that all men are equally endowed, for obviously there are wide divergencies in our abilities. Yet, when a man sees his own life and the lives of his brethren in the light of Christ, he feels no pride that he is superior to others in important respects. He remembers only that we who are strong must share the burdens of the weak; we who are wise must love the foolish; we who are rich must model our lives after the One who for our sake became poor.

There comes a time when the fate of a whole army rests not on the general, but on the private. There are occasions when the company makes a decisive impression not by words of the president, but by the actions of a clerk. More times than we can imagine, the Church has brought salvation not through the wise administration of the bishop, but through the humble ministry of the parish priest. Our interrelatedness makes salvation by a few supermen a vain hope. We rise or fall together, and we are members one of another. But this unity is found only in God and the reasons for it are all righteous ones.

In 1938 my wife and I went to England without any definite plan of travel. In Plymouth we met a man who was a city official and most kind and courteous in showing us about the city. One day we were on the Hoe, which is the high enbankment along the harbor, and he pointed out the Drake monument. The inscription read: "He blew his winds, and the ships were scattered." He then told us the story of one of the decisive naval battles of history. Drake, as I recall, was bowling on the Hoe when word was brought that the Spanish Armada had been sighted. It was one of the greatest fleets assembled up to that time. The superb and towering Spanish galleons must have struck terror to the heart of many an Englishman. But the small English ships with their intrepid captains went out to do battle. A stiff wind was blowing up the Channel. Then it was discovered that, while the smaller ships could be maneuvered to sail against the wind as well as with it, the cumbersome galleons could sail only with the wind and so were practically unmanageable. Drake and his men chased them up the Channel past Dunkirk, where they plunged on into the North Sea and around the coast of Scotland. Finally, they drove on to the Hebrides and were smashed to pieces.

Well, a people dominated by a superman philosophy is like the Spanish ships. They do well if they can sail when the wind is blowing them in the direction they want to go. But if it is necessary to veer to the right or left, or if the enemy is not solid and static, then comes disaster. It is disastrous when the success of the fleet depends on a few mighty, rigid ships. Much safer is the fleet with many maneuverable craft. Salvation is not from man, and to place our confidence in supermen is a delusion which will cost us our liberty.

2

The Delusion of Power

THE HEAD OF ONE OF OUR LEADING AIRPLANE COMPANIES, SPEAKING before a certain service club, gave a report on the situation facing America in the field of air defense. He described the growth of our Air Force and the probable air strength of the Russians. Then he made his main point: There is no such thing as a second-best air force. If your planes will reach an elevation of fifty thousand feet and your enemy's planes will reach fifty-five thousand feet, your fleet for all practical purposes is obsolete. It is like having a second-best hand in poker, he added.

Perhaps we have never been more aware of this truth than just now. We are power conscious and security minded. We throw the vast bulk of our resources into the search for national safety, but every advance seems to make us aware that the goal has moved even further away from us. Thoughtful men are beginning to ask if the kind of security we seek is obtainable and if power in the physical sense can offer what we want. Certainly it is true that in the very hour when we are stronger, militarily speaking, than at any other time in our history, we have suffered some of our biggest defeats. There seems to be more unfriendly criticism and more suspicion of our motives than at any time in our past. We have lost the friendship of millions of Asiatics. What is power? Is it anything more than the ability to get what we want? If so, what shall we say of our so-called power, on the one hand, and our frustration, on the other?

An English friend at the World Council of Churches Assembly in Evanston in the summer of 1954 told me of a strange experience.

He was taking a train for a speaking engagement, and an American friend learned of it. The American said he would be glad to drive the English visitor to the station, but he did not dare move his car and thereby lose his parking place. The Englishman asked me if it was not a commentary on our industrial civilization when a car became an object to fill and hold space along the side of a street rather than a means of transportation. Perhaps it is, and perhaps the whole question of power has become confused and obscure. What is it for and what is it supposed to do for us? Can it be that power is one of those delusions which, instead of preserving free-dom, may be the means of losing it?

I.   POWER IS A FACT

The universe is packed with power and power is one of the elements with which we must learn to deal. The continual march of science leads us to an ever-increasing appreciation of the mighty energy in things. Underneath the dead-appearing wastelands are the oceans of oil which turn the wheels of our industry. So far as our world is concerned, there is no death but only restless power.

All persons who have experienced an earthquake, have been made aware of the terrifying might underneath us. A few years ago I experienced a severe quake in Oregon, and it gave me a new sense of the fear that strikes at men when the earth itself seems insecure. In my office in a downtown building I was talking with a young preacher. I had been called to the telephone at the moment when the building began to sway. A crack came down the wall. I thought the building would crash, but the man at the other end of the line kept on talking and discussing the sensation. So, although scared, I was unable to think of a way to terminate the conversation and get to the street. When my friend finally hung up, the young preacher was nowhere in sight. Finding the elevator too slow, he had run down the stairs to the street. He said that he knew it was supposed to be women and children first, but he thought someone ought to go ahead and show them the way! Earthquakes are frightening because they reveal uncontrollable power.

A few years ago, I was in Japan visiting churches and schools. Days in Hiroshima and Nagasaki will never be forgotten, as survivors described the atom bomb attacks. When a Methodist minister, the Rev. Mr. Tanimoto, introduced us to a group of burned, scarred girls who had been through the experience, my feeling was shame and fear for the future. It was soon apparent that this secret of destruction in the atom could not be kept by our side, and now there are bombs that make these first ones look like children's toys. It is interesting that our fathers had too little and we have too much. We shall not die because we cannot control nature, but because we cannot control ourselves. We have more reservoirs of power which can be used for destruction than we bargained for.

In College Hill Cemetery, Lebanon, Illinois, there is a stone on the grave of Jennie E. Wilson, with this simple inscription:

> She was more to me
> Than I expected.[1]

That could be the epitaph of our civilization—we got more power than we expected.

What we have found in nature we find also in human society. This does not have to be argued when two great nations like America and Russia stand astride the world. "My head or thine" is the spirit of our day. But to some extent it has always been this way, for whether clothed in the language of diplomacy or stated in the blunt terms of threat and counterthreat, power groups are a fundamental reality in society. The dream of the liberals, who assumed a time of no conflict, is a vain one, and our experience indicates that we are destined to struggle forever.

The cities illustrate the same truth. On the surface a city's life may seem placid enough, but underneath the surface there is a constant battle for the control of its life. I never participated in the civic life of any community without having a fresh appreciation for those who fight for civic decency. It is a fight, constant, hard, and exhausting. Let the champions of righteousness doze for a moment, and the victories fade away. Reform movements usually are short-lived because they make the mistake of assuming a permanent victory. There is only a continual struggle, and the issues are only temporarily decided. Good intentions are not enough, and a general, vague hope that things will turn out right is the best ally that crooked politicians can desire.

The Christian ought to be forewarned against any of the sentimental nonsense that entraps the secular humanist. He knows all about sin and he remembers what happened to his Lord. The Prophets still speak to us, because we are the same kind of people to whom they spoke originally. They never tried to make people believe that entrenched evil could be removed with sermons and admonitions. They understood that such power as evil commands can be met only by the power of God. They were surrounded by empires and they knew what invasion meant. The early Christians were under no delusions concerning the power of the Roman state, and they would have been overwhelmed with despair if they had not had a revelation of One who was the power of God.

There is an old Irish cookbook that contains a famous recipe for rabbit stew. I like the way it begins: "Step 1—Catch your rabbit."[2] And if we are to live in this world and have any realistic perception of its nature, step one is to recognize the fact of power.

2. POWER CORRUPTS

There is hardly a more trite thing to say. But, while we understand this in relation to other people, we ignore it for ourselves. If truth would strike us personally as easily as it does generally, we would soon improve ourselves and our life.

It is also a very easy and prevalent thing to mistake ends and means, or to interchange them. This is the special temptation for a generation with no eternal point of reference. Perhaps this is the chief tragedy that relativism makes inevitable.

Take administration as an example. Any organization or association must have a certain amount of machinery connected with it, and an institution of any importance must be able to command the services of first-rate administrators. The artistic temperament may resent this and regard it as an enemy of all creative work, but the single inspiration is nearly always lost if it is not conserved by organization. Yet the administrator is ever in danger of regarding administration as an end in itself. Not so! Just to keep the machinery running smoothly is not the reason for an organization's existence. On the contrary, the machine exists to enable the institution to accomplish its real aims. How sad it is to see a man who no longer believes that administration is little more than a means to a larger goal.

A free people must be constantly alert to the encroachment of the philosophy that the government is an end rather than a means of service. As government grows in size, a subtle danger increases as many come to think that people exist to serve it. But if the government ceases to be a servant it becomes an idol. In some circles the term "welfare state" has an unpleasant connotation, but actually when the state ceases to be concerned primarily with the welfare of its citizens it becomes the great beast of *Revelation*. This does not mean that a government must do for people what they ought to do for themselves, but only that it must act always to prevent exploitation and establish justice.

There is in the exercise of power something that acts like a drug, giving delusions of grandeur. The nation, whether it be Rome, Spain, England, or America, finds the greatest difficulty in becoming powerful and still keeping clear its proper role.

The problem facing a secular society like ours is that often we have nothing to promise except more gadgets and an even higher standard of living. These are not sufficient reasons for a people to live by in times of stress. There comes a time when another million dollars is of little significance to the multimillionaire. The delusion that material progress for ourselves is a sufficient reason for great sacrifices is beginning to catch up with us.

I remember something a guide said to me in Rome. He described and explained the glory of the past and then he said that the Roman Empire fell because the Romans took too many baths. That seemed a strange idea to one who had been taught that cleanliness was next to godliness, and I asked him to explain further. The luxury of the baths came to be an end in itself, he commented, and the ruling class would not give them up to serve the nation either on the frontier or as administrators in the colonies. They wanted only their baths and their slaves. When a people uses its power and wealth to create more and more comfort, the end is in sight.

A few years ago in Manila, I was invited to attend a meeting of the Protestant youth on the campus of the University of the Philippines. There were about seventy-five students present and as I spoke to them, it seemed that there was an almost electric spirit of expectancy and spiritual vitality. I asked the young man sponsoring the group what caused this spirit, and he said it was because they were a minority group. Many of them, he went on, came from homes utterly unsympathetic to their joining the Protestant Church, and a few of them had gone through real persecution. All of them were aware that they stood under the close scrutiny and judgment of the Catholic majority, so that their religion meant a great deal to them. For them, it meant decision, commitment, choice. It came to me then, that the dangerous time for the church is when it becomes too powerful and yields to the temptation to depend on external influence rather than on inner strength.

When men begin to exhibit the "unconscious arrogance of conscious power," they are on the threshold of trouble. Pride is the fundamental sin, and it does not go unpunished. Jesus' word is the right one here: "For what does it profit a man, to gain the whole world and forfeit his life?" (Mark 8:36) Suppose that a man is so successful and powerful that he can obtain the whole world for himself. If in the process he loses his soul and the center of his life, the success is failure, for he has lost the essential treasure. It is this lust for power which blinds us to the difference between purposes and processes.

3. POWER MUST BE USED

The dangerous nature of power makes many a Christian suspicious of it in any form or place. There are those who seem to assume that the use of any kind of force is evil. A man's life, they seem to believe, is supposed to consist of a neutral harmlessness. There was an old Scotswoman who said she thought a certain young man would make an excellent minister because "he was a right harmless laddie." I have a great respect for the pacifists, but I have no admiration for the passivists. The two are quite different.

We have been told of all the harm that we can do if we act without complete knowledge and understanding. No doubt there is truth in this, but if it becomes an excuse for doing nothing in any circumstance, it is an evil doctrine. It is also unrealistic and impossible. For we have to act on the basis of inadequate knowledge a hundred times a day, and there is no way to get through life without being confronted by the fork in the road. This is the truth grasped by the existentialists—at least some of them. Life is ever throwing us onto the horns of dilemmas, and somehow we must get off the horns and act.

This is no plea for unconsidered action, but a facing of the truth that power must be used and will be used by someone. Life is more the result of many smaller choices and minor skirmishes than of just a few major choices. To do nothing is to do much for good or ill. And life will not wait. You cannot store electricity and use it at your convenience, for to save it is to lose it. This urgency is a part of the essential nature of human existence.

We have had an illustration of what happens to well-meaning people who believe that nothing need be done if your heart is right. After the war we brought our military forces home as quickly as possible and left empty places in Europe and the Orient which became vacuums. We awoke with a start to discover that no vacuum will last very long, for into it will flow some power to fill the emptiness. The Communist successes during the following years were in large measure due to our misunderstanding of this principle. We have had to learn the hard way that, if our power is not present, their power will be. Realistic political thinking begins with the assumption that empty places must be filled.

The city's life is the same. The complaints made by the good people are often unjustified. They complain that the worst elements seem to control the city government and that, subsequently, vice has too much influence in determining policy. But what they do not face is their own failure to offer anything to replace what they decry. Communities will not operate on a neutral basis. They are directed and shaped by forces which exert pressure. If men are too busy to spend time on their government, or if they are unconcerned, then those who will take the time and are interested will have their way. It is about as simple as that.

One of our difficulties is the false dichotomy we have established regarding the material and the spiritual. Too many of us have the idea that the spiritual is the vague, the indistinct, the otherworldly, and the sentimental. We cannot believe that the spiritual man will soil his hands with earthy matters, nor will he allow the things of the world to touch him. But the truly spiritual is tough and realistic. It is at home in the world and it works in the world. The spiritual man is not only concerned about the long future and the general welfare, but he is concerned with the immediate future and the situation next door.

Gandhi is the best modern example of the spiritual man using power. His methods were different than Stalin's, but his goal was the creation of a great nation and the attainment of freedom for a people. Few men exerted more power than the frail saint and few, if any, in our time exhibited more common sense and realistic appreciation of political facts. We must do away with the false idea that to be spiritually minded is to be naïve or impractical. Martin Luther spoke a good word for us when he said that you cannot rule the world with a rosary.

I have a friend who went into politics with almost as high a sense of calling as I felt on going into the ministry. He has devoted himself bravely and consistently to good causes, and his character is above reproach. I asked him one time how he was enjoying his work, and he said that it brought him some disillusionments, chief of which was the uncertain support a politician might expect from good people. He said they seem to weary of supporting an honest man long before bad people weary of supporting dishonest ones. He gave me chapter and verse for his feeling. He concluded that it was not the entrenched evil which was the problem, but the wavering concern of decent citizens for clean, economical government.

The Church is ever face to face with this reluctance. Christianity ought to be in the arena and not on the side lines only. The number of churchmen who assume that a good Christian is nothing more than a solid, conservative American is astounding. The number of people who are afraid that criticism of the Church's message of justice for all men will weaken the Church is discouraging. Since the days of Amos, there have been many champions of the institutions of religion who are actually afraid of the power of religion in society.

Yet if the power is kept in check, the institution itself dies. Reports from Eastern Germany tell of full churches at the worship services and reveal a deep spiritual hunger which the Communists never can destroy. But the youth programs are hampered, and the message must be innocuous so far as any prophetic word is concerned. Even our most careful Christian defenders of the status quo would soon tire of such an emasculated form of the Church. The young people I met in Scandinavia did not look to the state church as the challenge to their best work, but looked toward the state itself as the best place for social service. A church which lets itself get pushed aside from the main stream of social development will die. You cannot pickle the truth, nor can you embalm a dream. Young men will see visions and old men will dream dreams, and if they cannot find encouragement and opportunity to realize them through the Church, they will seek another field for their work.

When one of Bernard Shaw's colleagues resigned from Parliament rather than compromise, Shaw said:

When I think of my own unfortunate character, smirched with compromise, rotted with opportunism, mildewed with expediency, blackened by ink contributed to Tory and Liberal newspapers, dragged through the mud of Borough Councils and Battersea elections, stretched out of shape with wire pulling, putrefied by permeation, worn out with twenty five years pushing to gain an inch here and straining to stem a backrush there, I do think Joe might have put up with just a speck or two on those white robes of his for the sake of the millions of poor devils who cannot afford any character at all because they have no friends in parliament. Oh, these moral dandies, these spiritual toffs! these superior persons! Who is Joe anyhow that he should not risk his soul occasionally like the rest of us.

The Church and Christians must be in the thick of the battle and they must exercise power at the point where the moral and human decisions are being made.

4. POWER OF THE SPIRIT

What has been said does not imply that a church must get into politics or become simply another pressure group which tries to attain certain specific political ends. It does imply a church exerting a spiritual and moral influence in the arena of political and economic affairs. It assumes a powerful champion for all human rights, and a mighty defender of every human dignity.

Does all this sound unreal, idealistic? Do we really believe that spiritual power is any match for material might? P. A. Sorokin, the Harvard sociologist, whose life has hardly been a bed of roses, has dared to make a careful examination of what he calls *The Ways and Powers of Love*. His book is a testimony of what love and good-will have done in the rough-and-ready conflicts of life. He concludes that love is a power which is unequaled, and that a proper understanding of it would change the world. Love does not require that everyone become a saint, but as he puts it:

If the bulk of ordinary mortals would simply abstain from murdering other human beings; if they would cut in half their daily actions of hate and would double their daily good deeds, such a modest improvement in their moral conduct would enormously increase the output of love and decrease the output of hate, and thereby the general ethical and social level of humanity would be raised to a much higher level.[3]

Some men have learned that faith in God is the source of a tremendous power. Any age without faith is essentially a trivial age, and the man without faith has no firm foundation and no adequate goal. Professor William E. Hocking reported a conversation with a psychiatrist who was sincerely interested in understanding what religious men believe. He said that if in the miscellaneous events of the world one discerned a trend, then a man could be either for it or against it. This he conceded could make a great difference in the way a man lived. Professor Hocking agreed that this was the heart of religion, and that the saints' passion for right living was conceived as a cosmic demand. The psychiatrist said there was nothing unscientific in such an idea and then added, "Strange that such a simple thing should make so very much difference."[4]

But this simple thing goes to the root of the matter. It is the assurance that there is a more than human power making for right-eousness, and a purpose which commands and ennobles every human life. The universe holds us up, and the stars in their courses fight for us. The moral law is the unbreakable framework of all our striving, and we are held steady by a power which no tyrant can defeat. The stubborn might of great beliefs is at once our protection and our inspiration. Two Hollywood actresses were talking, when one of them referred to her horoscope. Said the other, "I did not know that you believed in astrology." "Oh", was the reply, "I believe in everything a little bit." And you could hardly find a better analysis of one of our chief ills—we believe in many little things a little bit, but we have no great faith in the power of God's revelation in Christ. We are the victims of every panacea and half-baked solution to the problems of men, and we exhibit as much superstition as African tribesmen. For we, like them, are idolators and not worshipers of the one true God.

We are face to face with issues which can only be rightly concluded by the power of the spirit. Our problems are basically religious and they must find spiritual solutions. Against the terror of the dehumanized materialisms running loose in the world, we must pose the kind of power which sent the early Christians to their struggle against the world.

The power we need is the power of the personal witness of what God can do. If you read the New Testament with any perception, it becomes clear that the writers put much stress on witnessing. They talk about eyewitnesses and they are content with nothing less than the testimony of men who can say, "I know, because I saw." Thus, in the book of Acts, the requirements in choosing a successor for Judas are clearly set forth:

So one of the men who have accompanied us during all the time that the Lord Jesus went in and out among us, beginning from the baptism of John until the day when he was taken from us—one of these men must become with us a witness to his resurrection. [Acts 1:21-22]

This transforming power of the gospel will alone suffice as the saving answer to our dilemmas. We must have not only the power to destroy, but also the power to build, to change, to plan. We need the power to become what we must be in order to create peace and goodwill. Again it is in Christ that the answer to our need is found. The Fourth Gospel puts it clearly: "But to all who received him, who believed in his name, he gave power to become children of God" (John 1:12). This power to become what we must be, so that our life may be ordered in harmony with God's will, is peculiarly the gift of Jesus Christ.

At the end of the Second World War, some of the speeches of Sir Winston Churchill were published under the title *The End of the Beginning*. In one of those great addresses Churchill, commenting on a speech of Hitler, said:

The most striking and curious part of Hitler's speech was his complaint that no one pays sufficient attention to his victories. Look at all the victories I have won, he exclaims in effect. Look at all the countries I have invaded and struck down. Look at the thousands of kilometers that I have advanced into the lands of other people. Look at the booty I have gathered, and all the men I have killed and captured. Contrast these exploits with the performances of the Allies. Why are they not down-hearted and dismayed? How do they dare to keep up their spirits in the face of my great successes and their many misfortunes?

And then there comes this great sentence:

He sees with chagrin and amazement that our defeats are but stepping-stones to victory, and that his victories are only the stepping-stones to ruin.

We cannot live without power. To lift the fallen takes power; to protect the innocent demands police power; to defend the nation requires military power. But the one Man in all history who could have been trusted with any kind of power made perfectly clear that power belongs to God and can be used only under His control. Whenever we forget that, our victories lead to an ultimate defeat; but when we remember, even our defeats will lead us to the ultimate victory.

3
The Mass Mind

IT HAS BEEN POINTED OUT BY JOSEPH WOOD KRUTCH IN THE *Saturday Review* that hobbyhorses are hard to obtain. A shopper for the *New Yorker* made some inquiries as to the reason, and found that the play-school consultants disapprove of hobbyhorses because they do not develop the group spirit. A child may gallop off on some lonely adventure and, according to the experts, that is bad. Apparently it is no longer recommended that youngsters should be encouraged to do what they want to do. Rather, they are to be guided into group adjustment.

It is amazing that this doctrine, so dear to the hearts of Communists, should have infiltrated into our way of life. For totalitarianism of any sort has this common mark, that it abhors difference and worships conformity. Theoretically, at least, we have always been in favor of individualism, and the "goose-step" spirit of our enemies has been one of our main objections to them and their way.

This spirit of forcing all things into a common pattern has interpenetrated much of our life. It is expressed in our minimizing of moral law, as well as in the learned nonsense spoken by behaviorists. It is the kind of doctrine that grows rapidly when men forsake the common sense of their experiences for intellectual theorizing. It is one of the delusions under which the people surrender their liberties, to use Edmund Burke's phrase.

1. CONFORMITY'S ATTRACTION

One of the rude awakenings experienced by my generation came when we saw the success of ways of life which denied so much of what we thought men wanted. In my youth no one doubted that democracy was invincible, precisely because it gave men what men craved above all else: liberty, individualism, responsibility, privacy, honored minorities. One heard stories about Russia but, after all, the Russians were headed in our direction, according to the speeches and words they published. Hitler could never get very far, we thought, for *Mein Kampf* was a hodgepodge of contradictions, false generalizations, and denials of what all right-thinking men believed. Practically in one man's lifetime, we have seen the climate of theology, politics, science, philosophy, change as a result of the tragic indications of new depths of evil in men.

We have had to change our minds about man's nature, even more than about the extent of evil. Emotion plays a much bigger part in our activity than the rationalists believed. Loneliness and emptiness are hard realities which for good or ill influence the behavior and the thought of persons. The Freudian emphasis on the power of the subconscious should have prepared us for some of the revolutions of our time. Men will worship something and find something of real or imagined worth to give their devotion to. Without a faith to live by, men will surrender easily to brutal authority.

The goal of tyranny is always conformity. If there is one thing it fears, as if it were the devil, it is the man who will not fit into a common mold or refuses to keep silent about his beliefs.

Many an American believes that such things might happen elsewhere, but not here. The gradual change in our spirit fails to impress the bulk of the population, and it is easy to understand now why people can lose their liberty without being aware of what is happening to them. Jane Addams of Hull House fame once remarked that there are not more fools in America than in other countries, but over here they are organized. Which is to say that if we ever start on the road to serfdom we will probably go faster and more completely than a more leisurely people.

Crawford H. Greenewalt, president of E. I. Du Pont de Nemours

& Company, in a recent speech commented on a standard psychological testing sheet used widely in personnel work. He applied the questions to Benjamin Franklin and concluded that Ben would not do so well if he applied for a job today in American industry. Such questions as "Do you daydream?" would receive the wrong answer from Ben Franklin, and his answer to "Are you more entertained by books than by companions?" would have been quite unsatisfactory. Mr. Greenewalt goes on to say that in all probability Charles Goodyear, Elias Howe, and Thomas Edison would not come out too well either with these testing questionnaires. Society seems to be afraid of individuality in spite of its talk about free enterprise.

Even if it fails to teach anything else, education is bent on teaching adjustment. A best-selling novel, *The Dollmaker* by Harriette Arnow, tells of a Kentucky backwoods family which lived in Detroit during the war. The small boy in the family had a very unhappy time at school because he could not adjust properly to the new environment. He had worked on the farm and carried responsibility beyond his years. But when he told about his experiences the city children and the teacher were sure he was lying. The mother visited the teacher to learn the cause of her son's desperate unhappiness, but she found no understanding and was given a blunt warning that the boy should either conform or get out. Finally, the little boy ran away from home and went back to the old place. He was guilty of only one crime. He would not, or perhaps he could not, fit into the pattern.

It is quite plain now that one of the greatest hazards in government service is that some second-rate politician, with no other way to make his name heard by the public, may try to smear the characters of men who have liberal tendencies. We are not going back to the days of small government and few government employees. Whether we like it or not, we are destined to have big government and millions of people working for government agencies, political platforms and promises notwithstanding. It is of the greatest importance, that we should have first-rate minds serving us in this capacity, which will not be the case if we make it possible for only party hacks to work for the government and at the same time respect themselves. The popularity of conformity is not only a foreign phenomenon but, unfortunately, we have its domestic counterpart.

A Wisconsin newspaper sent out a reporter to get people's signatures on the preamble of the Declaration of Independence. Out of 112 persons asked to sign it, only one consented, while the others regarded it as dangerous and subversive. Perhaps it is, but I keep thinking of how such an attitude would have pleased George III in 1776. Men like John Hancock would not have signed the document with a flourish, saying "George the Third can read that without his spectacles." And, incidentally, we would have had no Declaration of Independence at all, and certainly no United States of America shaped from the beginning by the traditions of freedom for all men.

2. CONFORMITY'S BETRAYAL

A Methodist preacher who began his ministry in South Dakota, tells of the fearful effect the great flatland had on some of the early homesteaders. One woman, whose husband was working in the city while she satisfied the requirements of the law by living on their claim, told of praying for a "miracle of shape." She longed for something, a tree or a hill, to rise up. "But the land lay there motionless and flat."[1] There is a flatness of the spirit which has the same deadening, frightening effect as the prairie. Our most creative seers who have described mechanical civilizations of the future, like Aldous Huxley or George Orwell, have emphasized the monotony of such life in spite of all its scientific miracles and gadgets. The real wealth and color of a society lie not in external accomplishments but in the lives of the individuals it creates. A glittering room full of stodgy people is drab; but a plain room full of lives which sparkle is alight with joy and wonder.

A doctor once discussed with a friend a most interesting case he was treating in the Boston Psychopathic Hospital. The patient was a manic-depressive and alternated between moods of exhilaration and despondency. In his happy times, the man was writing some excellent poetry which had great promise. The doctor was of the opinion that if a cure was completed the patient might become stable, yet he would lose his poetical gifts which seemed dependent on the "divine frenzy" of his confident periods. Should he be restored to mediocrity or, for the sake of a possible great poet, should he be made to suffer periods of extreme depression?[2]

Is it too much to say that God faced that same decision when He created man? He could have made a creature amenable and docile, but He chose to fashion a creature free, often unpredictable, sometimes uncertain, but capable of divine aspirations and creative dreams. Here is the description of man from one of the brilliant minds of our time:

Man is not ascended from the apes; the apes are descended from, are degenerate forms of a "manling," a tarsier type that could walk upright. Man is not the "foetalization of the ape" but the retention and enlargement of some tarsoid form. He has specialized in unspecialization, and so we may say, as Dr. Hugh Miller of the University of California has put it, man is yet to become a species, i.e., confined in a special form. Man therefore is man, the master of all beasts and not only the crown but the promise of all life, because he has retained sensitiveness, the upright carriage and the open, exploratory tentative unspecialized hand.[3]

What this seems to mean is that at the very heart of man's nature there is something not to be tamed or contained. Conformity, then, when it becomes the ruling passion of a people, is an idol and a betrayer.

A nation loses its most valuable citizens when it tries to force creative men into uncreative roles. The triumph of the reactionary forces over the French Huguenots drove a part of the best of France into exile and destroyed a large part of her moral strength. We have been the gainers from so many such banishments, for America has held the door open for people seeking freedom and privacy. Our heritage has been great, though not always aristocratic, for the depressed and the disinherited sought refuge here and made their own individual contributions. It has worked reasonably well for over a hundred and fifty years. Does it seem sensible to deny this freedom now?

Theodore Parker, the nineteenth-century American preacher and reformer, described our beginnings and our spirit in these words:

> We are a rebellious nation. Our whole history is treason; our blood was attainted before we were born; our creeds are infidelity to the mother church; our constitution, treason to our fatherland. What of that? Though all the governors in the world bid us commit treason against men, and set the example, let us never submit.[4]

One wonders how such words from a modern pulpit would be greeted.

I sat next to the president of a large American corporation at a service club luncheon. In the course of the conversation, I endeavored to find out about his work and something of the problems facing a man in his key position. He spoke of a number of things and then he said that the main question had to do with rules and freedom. He pointed out that it was necessary to have a framework of principles within which the different plants and offices must function. But it was necessary also to encourage initiative and imagination on the part of men within the organization. To create a great bureaucracy with men bound by rules which made them cogs in a machine meant the death of leadership and finally the death of the corporation. American industry, he intimated, did not believe that blind conformity was the path to success.

The individual man who follows this path ceases to be a man. Imagine a person who makes conformity the rule of his life and carries it to its farthest conclusion. He never lets himeslf be different than is the contemporary fashion. He never stands with a minority. He never says no when others say yes. He makes becoming an incarnation of the average man his ambition. He would never think of standing before a community to say, "I accuse," or "I protest." Is this the picture of a man? Is it not rather a description of a creature that has ceased to be human?

The meaning of personality does not lie in the realm of the drab flatland of acquiescence. It stands forth on those splendid highlands of brave defiance, and its grandeur is discerned in the lonely vision of one man's mind. Men are social creatures, but they are not mere herd creatures. A man is the servant of his brethren, but his service is personal and it finds its direction in an ultimate loyalty to God. For a man to give his fellows what they want and always do what they want him to do is to destroy his integrity, which is the central citadel of personality.

There seems to be a tendency in our time to confuse goodness with inactivity, and wisdom with platitudes. So often the self-appointed guardians of the Republic try to freeze society in the name of saving it. If a thing is alive, it will not be possible to preserve it negatively, for life means growth. An inordinate emphasis on conformity is the sure sign of weariness, of age, and of approaching death.

3. POWER OF DIVERSITY

Perhaps no one believes this more than a Methodist, for his whole tradition has been one of itineracy and change. In a letter to a friend in 1756, John Wesley put down his feeling about settled pastorates:

Be their talents ever so good, they will ere long grow dead themselves, and so will most of them that hear them. I know, were I myself to preach one whole year in one place, I should preach both myself and most of my congregation asleep. . . . No one whom I yet know has all the talents for beginning, continuing, and perfecting the work of grace in one whole congregation.[5]

This is rather an extreme point of view, and most churches seek the kind of minister who can stay in one place a long time. But there is much to be said for a church's need of diversity and for the strengthening influence of a change of emphasis.

Diversity encourages growth. The American way of life, which means so many different things to different people, is certainly a mixed way. We are not a doctrinaire people who prefer to fit our methods into a preconceived pattern. This is something so many people fail to appreciate, but even a hasty glance around us will reveal that we do not hesitate to use methods which are often inconsistent with each other.

We send our telegrams by way of a private corporation, but we send our letters by a government postal service. I heard a man argue that we ought to take the mail service away from the government and hand it over to a corporation. I do not think many Americans will agree with him. Teachers are community employees but doctors are rugged individualists. Roads are built by the state, but rails are laid by private companies subject to certain state regulations. In the same city you may find electricity sold by both private and public utility companies. Everyone subscribes to the philosophy of free enterprise, but where are the men who will refuse government subsidies for farm products, hospital construction, or education?

Now, this is not mentioned with any idea of ridiculing our way of life, but only to point out that too much of our nationalistic oratory simply ignores the diversity of America. We are a sectionalized nation, as any man knows who travels about it. The South is different from the North and both sections have difficulty at times in understanding and appreciating each other. The East often irritates the West, and vice versa. One finds different accents, varying customs, diversified standards. Yet I have never found a man who suggested that we would be better off if there were two or more separate nations within our boundaries, nor has anyone ever suggested that our staying together was a mistake. We have had to follow the path of compromise and checks, but our diversity has been strength and not weakness.

In our present conflict with communism, our approach has tended to be a sort of "me tooism." They promise this much, we will promise even more; they will grant you these advantages, but we will double the offer. We ought to take seriously the remark of a French editor who said, what he feared most of all was not what separated America and Russia, but what they have in common. We have failed in the flood of hysteria and fear which has surrounded us, to make plain to the world wherein we differ from the Communists.

It is this diversity that is fundamental, and if men have a deep desire to be themselves without facing persecution by a secret police or brainwashing by party propagandists, then in heaven's name let us offer them these liberties. William Faulkner wrote an interesting article with this significant title: "On Privacy the American Dream: What Happend to It?"[6] On the basis of his own experience and observation, the Nobel Prize author maintained that this part of our heritage is being destroyed. One of the horrors of communism is that it allows no privacy and so turns the state into a prison. If in the name of security or publicity we should destroy this precious possession, it will be a fatal loss.

Diversity not only encourages growth, but it fosters creativity. There is a sense in which the sign of life is conflict and we should be suspicious of too much unanimity. Controversy is the mark of intellectual life, and those who would turn our universities into indoctrinating factories betray their preference for safe death to dangerous life. And the same is true of the Church.

We have heard a great deal in these days about the scandal of the divisions within the Christian Church. This, for the most part, is a healthy sign of our desire to unite Christians against an evil world, and it indicates a sense of the true spirit of Christ. Yet it sometimes assumes that all differences are automatically sinful, which I cannot accept. Like the poet, I thank God for all dappled things.

There is an evil competition which has had its way too much with the churches, and there can be no apology for it. It is stupid and wasteful to have four churches in a small community where there ought to be only one; we bring discredit to the whole Christian enterprise. But the new Protestant strategy of comity agreements is the answer to this foolishness, and the great body of Protestant Christianity has grown up to this more statesmanlike approach.

I believe in a reasonable amount of healthy pressure and godly competition. When the Congregationalists a mile or two down the street are getting ready to make their youth program more effective and attractive, the Baptists and the Methodists have to examine their own programs and make some improvements. That is all to the good. Any denominational success strengthens and encourages all of us.

If organic unity is the final goal, then the state church would seem to be the answer. There are countries where something like 95 per cent of the people are nominal members of one church. This is unity with a vengeance. That such churches have something we do not have is quite apparent, and there can be no doubt that they symbolize something very precious in the life of the nation. But I have yet to find such a church that impresses me with Christian vitality and social effectiveness. As a matter of fact, and this sounds like boasting, where does one find a more vital church life than is found in the United States? Where do people go to church in greater numbers? Where does the Church dare to speak more prophetically? And where are more children and young people involved in church programs? Any man knows that there is much wrong with us, and in terms of what God has a right to expect of

American Christianity we are woefully lacking. But the free church tradition of the Western democracies seems to have justified itself in terms of relevancy and, to me at least, it symbolizes not weakness but strength.

I cannot refrain from expressing my personal sense of debt to the various Christian traditions and communions. My education was given me by a Methodist college and two Congregational theological seminaries. My wife was a Presbyterian. Brethren and Disciple ministers have been my dearest friends and colleagues. Catholic laymen and priests have inspired and illuminated my imagination. One of my favorite pulpits is a Unitarian church in Pennsylvania. Let us by all means come closer together in our Councils of Churches, both local and national, but let us glory in, and perhaps boast a little of our diversities, which provide a fellowship for every man regardless of his theological or temperamental tendencies.

Katherine McAfee Parker wrote a brief life of her father, Dr. Cleland Boyd McAfee, and told of a time when her sister Ruth had gone to college and had her faith shaken. Ruth wrote home and told her father that she thought he ought to know that she was not certain about a number of things concerning God, Christ, the Bible, and what people ought to do. "I'm not sure of anything," she wrote, "I'm sorry to tell you this, but you ought to know." To her surprise and disappointment, her father wrote back that he was delighted with her letter for it showed for the first time that she was thinking. He urged her to go ahead and study further and use all her mind.[7]

Something of this happens to the Protestant who meets other men with other interpretations who challenge his own position. It allows some of the secondary matter to blow away and it reveals the substantial. To sharpen our thought on other traditions makes us more appreciative of the breadth, the depth, and the height of the Christian faith.

4. MEANING OF UNITY

Associate Justice Felix Frankfurter, of the United States Supreme Court, gave this definition of our American unity:

> Ours is the only country in the world's history where men are bound together not by a common territory, not by a common racial source, or a single body of theological beliefs. We are bound together by a sense of the ultimate simple decency of human dignity. Nothing binds us together but this sense of frail, fallible, aspiring human beings.[8]

This is a universal principle, for unity is always of the spirit. We do not succeed in creating real unity through coercion, organization, pressure, but only by finding a common object of trust, loyalty, and devotion.

Men are unified when they respect one another. This is a quality which is not for sale nor is it amenable to force. One of the best examples in my experience is the Council of Bishops of the Methodist Church. There are thirty-seven of us in the United States. I doubt that you could assemble an equal number of more rugged individualists. Whether that is the kind of man elected to the office as a rule or whether the office transforms men into such a pattern, I do not know. But they are different! They come from different sections of the country with differing traditions. They have various backgrounds and educational experiences. Their theologies are personal and their outlooks on political and social matters are often in conflict. Yet there is a fellowship among the members of the Council that is one of my most precious possessions. We do not always agree, but we never cease to love and respect one another. Of such is the kingdom of unity!

This generation has been led astray by a failure to determine the difference between heresy and subversion.

Any American has a right to be a heretic, for there is no orthodoxy of politics, economics, or religion to which we can force submission. We have some weird interpretations in these and other fields of thought, but we have believed it better to welcome all free expression and trust to the judgment of the people. An American has no right to be subversive, which means to corrupt or betray, or seek to overthrow. But in the framework of loyalty to the nation, Americans have the right to their own vagrant ideas and beliefs.

Differing denominations may be more unified than a state church if they respect one another's integrity and goodwill. One of the great experiences of my Christian life was the meeting of the General Assembly of the Presbyterian Church in Los Angeles. I have felt the lift of the World Assembly of the Disciples of Christ and my Greek Orthodox brethren have more than once fed my spirit. I have no intention of leaving my own denomination, for it is in a special sense home to me. But there is not the slightest desire in my heart to have all people join one church.

We are brought together by the power of faith. We believe in God and, though we may not be able to sum up that faith in one single creed, still we stand on a common foundation. We believe in men, for the Bible is the cornerstone of what we call Western civilization. We believe in truth and its judgment on all falsehood and its final victory over all lies. We believe in persons and not systems, freedom and not slavery, goodness and not brutality. Unity is a spiritual reality and it is only wounded and hindered by a lust for conformity. It was summed up by a sentence by John Steinbeck inscribed on a gift to John O'Hara: "The lonely mind of one man is the only creative organ in the world and any force which interferes with its free function is the Enemy."

When in the sixteenth century a German monk spoke and wrote against certain practices of the Church, he did not begin with any large ideas of changing the social order or starting a revolution. Others took up the publicizing of his theses and they soon became the talk of Germany, for they struck a responsive note. Luther's unexpected emergence as a reformer was in the same category as Karl Barth's experience. He described himself as a man climbing a winding staircase in the steeple of an ancient cathedral. In the darkness he reached out to steady himself and took hold of a rope. He was startled to hear the clanging of a bell.[9]

When Luther was called to Worms in April, 1521, he faced the Emperor and a representative of the Pope. After some general discussion, he was commanded to make a plain answer to the demand that he recant. Then came his fateful words:

Since then your Majesty and your lordships desire a simple reply, I will answer without horns and without teeth. Unless I am convicted by Scripture and plain reason—I do not accept the authority of popes and councils, for they have contradicted each other—my conscience is captive to the Word of God. I cannot and I will not recant anything, for to go against conscience is neither right nor safe. God help me. Amen.

That was the beginning of the Protestant Reformation and its emphasis on each man's priesthood and dignity. It was the foundation of the separation of church and state and of the insistence that a man's conscience is the court of last appeal. It was the affirmation that governments must respect the relationship between a man and God. It was, in short, the proclamation of freedom which must never be subordinated to conformity. There are so many of the values of our way of life which have their roots in that heroic struggle against authoritarianism, and we rejoice that we are the spiritual children of the Reformation.

II

DESIGNATIONS

II

DESIGNATIONS

4

Pilgrims

THE BIBLE IS AGAINST THE KIND OF LIFE THAT IS SETTLING DOWN. It is critical of any view which assumes too much permanence on this earth. It is opposed to any assumption that treasures on earth are adequate values for men to strive after. The Bible holds up a continual warning against inordinate desire for permanency. There is a sense in which it is proper to take literally the opening words of Jesus' famous parable of the talents: "For the kingdom of heaven is as a man travelling" (Matt. 25:14, King James).

The book of Hebrews assumes that men are strangers and exiles on this earth. It tells the story of the great heroes of the faith who lived in terms of expectation and pleased God so that He prepared for them a city, and was not ashamed to be called their God. To the author of this book, the sure sign of a true son of God is a willingness to live as a stranger here with an eye on the true homeland of the spirit. The unreligious man takes the world too seriously and regards it as too permanent, while the religious man knows that this is not his home and is ever aware of its impermanence.

It is suggestive that John Bunyan titled the greatest Christian allegory *Pilgrim's Progress*. In the opinion of that seventeenth-century Christian, the life of the follower of Christ is a journey. A book written a few years ago by George F. Willison described the kind of people who settled America as *Saints and Strangers*. Some of these colonists were religious men, called the Pilgrims. Surely one of the marks of the Christian is this spirit of march and a refusal to settle down in some safe situation where the chief problem is maintaining a status quo. One of the names for Christians

47

is Pilgrims, and America today still needs the spirit of the Christian pilgrim.

I.   RETURN TO YESTERDAY

We ought to recognize at the beginning that there is always a human urge to return to a past paradise. We are like the Italian woman once described by William James. She sat on the sidewalk in New York handing out cards which said she had come to America to raise money to return to Italy. The pull of some rosy memory of yesterday is the strongest force in the lives of many people.

The Old Testament story of the Garden of Eden has many a significant meaning, and one of them concerns what happened after Adam and Eve were expelled. You remember they sinned and were driven forth into a hard world, sentenced to earn their bread by the sweat of their brow. And God made it clear to them that there was no returning. "He drove out the man; and at the east of the Garden of Eden he placed the cherubim, and a flaming sword which turned every way, to guard the way to the tree of life" (Gen. 3:24).

There must have been many times in the days following when Adam and his wife longed desperately to go back to that idyllic existence in the Garden. In the midst of their hard work and their bitter experiences, the past life must have haunted them with its ease and beauty. But they could never forget the angel and the flaming sword, and God's anger. In their human experience they had reached the point of no return, as all men do at the close of every day. To know freedom is to know that every garden of experience, both sweet and bitter, is guarded against our going back.

I was born in a little town in northern Michigan, but my family moved to California before I was five. My parents talked about places I could remember only dimly, but I pictured them as a kind of fantasy land or dream country. Twenty-five years later my wife and I drove up through Michigan to see the wonderful villages of my childhood. It was a mistake! The country had been lumbered off, leaving a countryside of stumps and poor farms. Some of the towns were nearly deserted, and the buildings were often unpainted and in the last stages of dilapidation. I wished that the pictures of my imagination had been left unmarred.

Too many people, especially in America, have a great nostalgia for youth. One of the most pitiable figures I know is the woman who cannot adjust herself to the inevitable fact that she is growing older. Men are sometimes the victims of this sickness, but it seems to me more of a feminine delusion. Such a woman dresses like a schoolgirl, talks like a teen-ager, acts like a debutante, and fools no one but herself. She is ridiculous, but also sad in her foolishness. When a woman or a man is not afraid of age, that person often attains a dignity and a beauty which more than compensates for youth.

An unhappy youth may have certain compensations as the years pile up. I have never wanted to go back to adolescence and I am glad that those early years are past. Where did the nonsense arise that young people are always happy? Those were some of the unhappiest of all my days, and life to me grows more marvelous, more exciting, and more satisfying with every passing year. It is probably easier for some of us to escape this lust for a return to youth than it is for others. But, easy or hard, we had better escape it.

A people can be captured by false promises of returning to normalcy or going back to some previous condition remembered as much better than the present. Toynbee speaks of the failure of a civilization to respond to challenge as the beginning of the end. It is the spirit of ignoring or postponing the decisions which the times demand we face. If we have made wrong choices in our national life, and we have, those choices are now a part of our life and it is impossible to circle around them and go back to the period before they were made. We have to live with them and move forward toward wiser policies which must take into account what we have done and what we have become. A call to freedom is a demand that we shall be unbound by the past.

Thomas Wolfe's title, *You Can't Go Home Again,* is a good one. When we speak of going home we mean a getting back on the right road. The Prodigal Son went back to his father to get his bearings again and establish the right relationships with his family and friends. But it would never have been just the same as when he left it, and he was not returning to some comfortable house where he might spend the rest of his days in static security. We get back on the strait and narrow way so that we may push forward once more.

There is something about Jesus' return to Nazareth which speaks to every man's experience. I wonder if he had not looked forward to that return with great expectation. He thought of the familiar places and the old friends he would see again. He had been wandering without home or kindred for a long time, and homecoming must have loomed large in his thought. But everything went wrong. The people would not listen because they could not comprehend. Instead of sympathy and love, he found suspicion and hatred. No, it was not Nazareth that was to be his goal, but Jerusalem.

The healing for many a man is to learn that standing before every past Garden of Eden is the angel and there is the flaming sword. The sooner we can learn that the hope of returning to some easier paradise of the past is vain and impossible the sooner we will learn how to live adequately and victoriously. Sometimes the psychiatrist must be called in to heal an extreme case of the backward look, but often the healing for Christians is to call them by their rightful name of Pilgrims. The gospel is a healing influence, because it turns us into strangers and exiles on the earth of whom "God is not ashamed to be called their God, for he has prepared for them a city." From the inability to escape the lure of past virtues and vices, may the good Lord deliver us.

You cannot cling to yesterday, and life must go on. Every paradise is guarded against our return, and we must seek the gardens of tomorrow. We can never return to America's yesterday. We must seek the promise of the future.

2. SETTLING WHERE WE ARE

Now, if there is an urge to return to yesterday, there is at times a natural desire to settle down just where we are. We many not want to go back to anything, but we do not want to go forward either. We are content to stay, for we like it here and we never had it better. This spirit is usually associated with age, though it is not necessarily lacking in younger people. There are such creatures as "young fogies" who are suspicious and fearful of anything suggesting reform, advance, or change. Walter Lippmann, in his undergraduate days, said, "Men who are 'orthodox' when they are young are in danger of being middle-aged all their lives." Yet, on the other side of the ledger, I have known old men who until the day they died dreamed and planned of new adventures, new projects, social and political improvements. We are speaking of an attitude of mind and a condition of the spirit rather than chronological age.

Jesus was against this stolid spirit and he opposed all who would freeze any religious or social situation. Perhaps the chief source of our information for this assertion is the Parable of the Talents. It is a teaching that goes against so much of the prudent, careful moralism that passes in our time for religious teaching. Better to risk, he is saying, what you have and lose it than to safely hide it away like a miser. There is a kind of divine carelessness about our Lord that goes against the grain of our contemporary ethics. As someone has put it, we do not ask what we shall do to be *saved*, but what shall we do to be *safe*? Jesus' kind of life was full of risk and movement, and its safety was in the realm of the spirit.

Or consider Jesus' opposition to the Pharisees and his criticism of their legalisms. He must have known the moral grandeur of much of Pharisaism, and he must have been aware of the purifying influence of those lovers of the Law. But over against certain undeniable virtues, there was the serious weakness of regarding religion as a finished affair. They were loyal, but their loyalty was to a system and not to the spirit of the living God. Because of this essential misunderstanding of the truth about God, they became His enemies and the object of Jesus' most bitter denunciations.

Now, Jesus was properly appreciative of the Law, and there is nothing in his teaching to show any innate disrespect for its contributions. But legalism, with its inevitable tendency to regard religion only as precept and demand, could not contain or encompass his revelation. There was so much more to know about God than the Law could tell, and so much more to experience than the Pharisee could describe. The Kingdom of Heaven could be entered now, but its fullness was out beyond, and its promise was so convincing that he made men believe the best was yet to be. Once men gave themselves to him, they became pilgrims seeking the city God had prepared for them; and so far as the earth was concerned, they were strangers and exiles.

This spirit of travel and adventure has been emphasized, some say exaggerated, in the Methodist connection. Bishop Francis Asbury, sometimes called "The Prophet of the Long Road," was always troubled when one of his young preachers wanted to get married. (I am troubled when they do not want to get married.) This first American bishop of the church knew that married men had a habit of asking for a settled parish on the east coast, and he wanted them ready to ride to the frontier settlements at a moment's notice. Asbury's idea was that a preacher of the gospel must have no settled habitation, but stand ready to follow any road or path if he could be sure there were people at the other end.

Such a spirit is impossible without faith. One can almost say that the test of Christian faith is whether or not a man is afraid of change. A desire to freeze a situation is a sure sign of inner fear and uncertainty about the trustworthiness of God. When we strive to protect ourselves against any fluctuation of conditions, preferring that everything remain just as it is, we are driven to attitudes of paganism and the support of policies which may be evil. That is not a proper goal for men and it is not a legitimate test of policy. It is the mark of doubt and faithlessness, while it may masquerade under the name of patriotism or worldly wisdom. It is neither!

The mark of the great age is exploration. It may be in the realm of nature and marked by men sailing into unknown seas to find unknown continents. Or it may be in the realm of political life as men burst the bonds of doctrines, like the divine right of kings, to find the human, democratic basis for the organization of their society. Or it may be the escape from a classical bondage by yielding to the spirit of science and crossing frontiers formerly regarded as boundaries. Or it may be breaking the barriers of legalistic religion to seek freedom for the human spirit through service to Christ, as in the case of the Reformation. But in whatever area it may take place, it is a striking of the tents and a moving forward, and it is essentially a spiritual affair. For the past nineteen centuries, whenever such a new burst of courage and energy has broken through artificial limits, seeking more abundant life, the influence of the Man of Nazareth is discerned. For, consciously or unconsciously, men have heard again the words of the Apostle: "For freedom Christ has set us free; stand fast therefore, and do not submit again to a yoke of slavery" (Gal. 5:1). Christianity has been the greatest influence for stirring men up that has ever appeared on the earth.

The current tendency to regard our religion as a mere bolsterer of the present is a complete misunderstanding of it. The number of prominent men who have shown a new interest in the Church, because they see it as an ancient institution capable of putting the brakes on change, is legion. And it is extremely unfortunate. Such people would make the gospel a mere guarantee that what they are and the way they want things to be have God's sanction. Yet if the gospel does not become a lash on our pride and fear, it becomes a man-made philosophy with neither healing nor power in it.

3. LIFE AS TRAGEDY

We can forget the truth that Christians are pilgrims, if we deny that this life is essentially tragic. Such a delusion we have been at great pains to create. A whole school of religious interpretation has grown up to deny that life is tragic, and by carefully selecting the material it gives the impression to the Biblically ignorant that Christianity is merely a success-cult. To such as these, the earth becomes home and success becomes the worthy goal of life. The uncritical and the unwary are led to believe that there is some magic formula that will eliminate their loneliness and set them free from their frustration and fear.

A day of trouble brings out the best and the worst. When the day of trouble corresponds with a day of doubt, the worst is a blindness which prefers pleasant pretense to unpleasant reality. For a generation that prides itself on its realism, we can believe more things that are not so than a superstitious jungle tribe. We can believe that wishing will make it so; or that if we ignore the unpleasant fact it will go away. We can pretend that all is well or that peace can be bought. We can talk ourselves into believing that science will soon come up with balm for a broken heart, or that soon we will have a psychological formula for a guilty conscience. But we will not believe that only heaven can heal the sorrows of earth. Somehow we try to assure ourselves that life confined to the earth can be made happy and satisfying.

We are great believers in drugs, and for good reason. The new wonder drugs have wrought miracles when it comes to killing infection and pain. We have a pill to take when we want to relax, and another one to swallow if we want to sleep. Still another one will keep us awake, and yet others will give us such a sense of well-being that we appear alert and sparkling. If we eat too much, there is, according to the advertisements, a pill which takes away all bad aftereffects. Cocktails, we are assured, will relax the tired businessman before dinner, and afterwards too. All in all, we have learned how to get us through the hours of the days either drugged or stimulated, according to our needs. We can deal with almost any problem except death, and we have even made a try in that direction.

Our method has been to ignore death by not talking about it, and we try to disguise everything that has anything to do with this unpleasant experience. We remind ourselves how life has been lengthened, and I should not be surprised if some moderns do not half expect science to offer a cure for dying. We will not say a man has died, but that he has passed to the great beyond or fallen into his eternal sleep. To say bluntly that so-and-so died would hardly be proper. The funeral service arranges the whole business in a pleasant manner for all except those who feel the great sorrow of parting from one long loved. The mortuary profession has made the funeral a work of art, and the tragic fact of death is hidden from the general public.

But the Bible will have nothing of this pretense, and it becomes almost embarrassingly blunt and frank about so many terrifying things in life. It begins with the worst and when it achieves the heights of hope it is only after descending into the depths of despair. It is shot through and through with the assumption that life is essentially tragic.

How invulnerable am I actually? Hardly at all! I live my life in the midst of danger and surrounded by the threat of accident. I can take all the precautions possible and get vaccinated against all the contagious diseases. But airplanes crash and automobiles collide, while the so-called acts of God make it quite plain that there is no hiding place down here. The Ninetieth Psalm is more than a sentimental poem when it speaks its profound human experience (vv. 5-6):

> Thou dost sweep men away; they are like a dream,
> like grass which is renewed in the morning:
> in the morning it flourishes and is renewed;
> in the evening it fades and withers.

What is permanent in this life? Not very much. The things I value grow old and wear out. Those I love grow old and die. Victories are not permanent, and my achievements are not final. The business I built can be swept away in a sudden reverse. That which I treasure here will be left behind, for moth and rust doth corrupt and thieves do break in and steal.

And what is the ultimate end of my life? It takes some time for the fact of death to have a personal meaning. Youth is a period of accepting mortality generally but never specifically. Yet soon or late there comes that momentous realization that we are no better than our fathers and death is our ultimate destiny. Stephen Vincent Benét, in a little poem entitled "Thirty-Five," indicated that this realization comes around that age.

Now, what is the real significance of all this? It means that life is essentially tragic, and that from the standpoint of this earth alone it has an unhappy ending. Paul could say that the last enemy to be overcome is death, but the man of this world only cannot say it. Death may be postponed by the use of our modern skill and wisdom, but it can never be eliminated. Someday I will die, and someday those I love the most will die. There is a parting at the end of the way and there is a cessation of my life at some rendezvous which I must keep.

Gutzon Borglum, who carved the Mount Rushmore Memorial, was asked if the faces were perfect in detail. He replied that the nose of George Washington was an inch too long, but that it will erode to exactly the right length in about ten thousand years. The

Executive Digest, which tells the incident, adds this admonition: "Have patience." All this is very well, but what is going to happen ten thousand years from now is not of much comfort to me. There may be some rare individuals who can be content in believing that things will go right in the long centuries of the future, but there are not many of us in that sublime category. A few uncertain years here, and then oblivion, strikes at our hearts with fear and frustration. All the books in the world on "how to be happy" will not get to the root of this problem if they deal only with this world.

4. OUR ULTIMATE DESTINATION

But if we cannot return, and we cannot stay where we are, and life confined to this earth is tragic, still the last word has not been spoken. There is a heavenly country and there is a city which God has prepared for us. Toward that eternal destination we travel with assurance and joy. This is the only healing homesickness, for it lightens the load and keeps us on the straight path. Men become like that new jet plane which "is equipped with a radar system that locks the plane onto the target in the dark." We will not always have a bright light on our path, but we will never get lost in the darkness. Without this goal fixed securely in our minds and hearts, we can never be sure that we are on the right road, but when it is accepted gladly and completely, we never get lost.

Now, this heavenly city does not make the present journey meaningless or drab. Quite the contrary! As St. Catherine put it so wisely, "All the road to heaven is heaven." The fear that a belief in the Other World leads to a lack of appreciation of this one is false. I venture to suggest that this world never reveals its true beauty until a man knows that he is a pilgrim traveling through it on his way to heaven. For until we are free from the worship of the false gods of this world, we cannot know the truth about it.

The business of growing old is inescapable and of greatest import. If we fail here we are doomed to much unhappiness as well as much needless pain. If we can learn how to grow old gracefully we have learned one of the essential lessons of triumphant living. The people who have learned this secret never have a sense of life running down, but of life stretching forward; not into the valley of death, but *through* that valley. The journey grows more interesting with every passing mile, and we can hardly doubt that the most interesting part of all will be on the other side of the grave. Old age can be bitter and sordid, but so can youth; it can be also as wonderful and glorious as the close of an October day. The first thing to know is that we are pilgrims.

The vision of that city which God has prepared for us teaches us how to enjoy passing wonders and the transient treasures without worshiping them. Christianity never encouraged any man to despise the world or to deny the gifts it contains for our pleasure. The Christian pilgrim has an increased sense of the fragile loveliness which surrounds him, and his wonder is heightened even as his ability to appreciate is made more sensitive. "This is our Father's world." But we are saved from pretending that the gods of this world are worthy of our worship, and we do not bow down before the work of our own hands.

The Christian pilgrim can part from his loved ones without despair. He cannot escape loneliness and profound sorrow when a beloved voice is silenced and a loving hand can no longer touch him. But it is the sorrow of parting which has a quality of purifying sweetness in it, and not the blighting despair that comes to those who have no further hope. We come to see that until we accept our status as strangers and exiles on this earth, moving toward that city which God has prepared for us, we are not prepared to live on the earth.

A Catholic priest named William Sullivan left his church when he felt his choice had to be made between the institution and the truth. He became minister of the First Unitarian Church of Germantown and had a great ministry in that pulpit. In his autobiography he stated in the Foreword the moral learned from his long and difficult experience. "So at the end of the long journey," he wrote, "I have come to this: the first article of my creed is that I am a moral personality, under orders."[1] What that man had learned about life was its mobility and its meaning. It was neither a dead end nor an aimless wandering, but a marching toward the heavenly city, conscious of God's demands and purposes for every human life.

The perspective of the pilgrim gives the true basis for choice. A man can hardly tell what is important and what is transitory on the basis of this world's standards. The disasters which overtake men and nations are so often the results of honest but false choices. Policies which brought darkness were sometimes promulgated by men who thought they would bring the light. How many times has our generation been deceived by the promises of false dawns. For when men have no eternal point of view, and are dealing with the merely temporal, they cannot even choose realistically or wisely. The man going on a journey has to strip things down to essentials, and he has to choose what is necessary. If he takes more along, he knows that they are the items which can be discarded when necessary. It is the traveler who knows freedom.

We need to be reminded who we are and where we are going. The book of Hebrews put it very clearly and, after reminding Christians that they are strangers and exiles so far as this earth is concerned, it gave them this wonderful assurance: "Therefore God is not ashamed to be called their God, for he has prepared for them a city." To put it in another way, God is proud of His pilgrims.

5
Priests

MOST CHRISTIANS IN OUR TIME WOULD BE SHOCKED TO BE THOUGHT of as priests. Whatever else they are supposed to be, this is a name they would regard as applicable to only a small segment of the Christian Church. For a priest is thought of as a professional servant of religion, and even then he is not too highly regarded in the Protestant tradition. It is, therefore, somewhat disconcerting to hear Peter address his generation of Christians as "a royal priesthood." There is probably no better illustration of the difference in viewpoint that has developed between the early Christians and those of the twentieth century.

The word "profane" did not originally mean cursing, or swearing, or what we usually call profanity. It meant "before the temple" or outside of the holy place. That is where the people could congregate, while only the priest could enter into the sacred dwelling of God. The profane life is really an unfenced kind of life where everything and everybody is admitted and welcomed. Peter, apparently, was telling those early Christians that they could go into the holy of holies since Christ had made them holy. They were people with a sacred calling and a high sense of the holiness of personality. They were redeemed from the wide-open, stained, tarnished, secularized life, which assumed that only certain men were to be chosen for the exercise of the priesthood.

The Reformation was a rediscovery of this long-hidden truth, and one of its fundamental principles was "the priesthood of all believers." Peter has usually been claimed as a kind of special saint belonging to the Roman Catholic tradition but, in this respect at least, he is entirely Protestant. The barriers between a professional ministry and the laity are ever in danger of being raised, even in the free churches. We need to go back constantly to the New Testament and to the Reformation for a clearing of our vision. Most Protestants need a new appreciation of the priestly functions of our religion, and we need to redefine what that function is for each man personally. Let us begin with the assumption that one of the names for Christians is *priest*, and see what some of the implications may be.

I. IN THE ROLE OF SERVANT

The priest is first of all a servant of God. He never doubts that his first obligation lies there and his ultimate loyalty must be to the One in whom we all live and move and have our being. Perhaps the unique qualities of the priest can be best clarified if we contrast him with the prophet.

The prophet is the more spectacular figure and in the long history of our Jewish-Christian heritage he has received the most notice and respect. That is as it should be, although it has been carried so far at times that the priest has had much less than his due. The prophet had very little respect for institutions as such. They seemed to him stodgy, mechanical, lifeless organizations, more interested in form than in life. Too often he was quite right in his judgment, for organized religion hardly ever escapes substituting ceremony for spiritual vitality. The prophet, therefore, is often outside the institution of religion, and its severest critic.

The prophet is a wanderer without a settled habitation or parish. He speaks his flaming word on the street or in the field, but seldom does he preach a series of sermons in a church. He has a terrible sense of justice and does not hesitate to proclaim what justice demands and what forces or persons are standing in the way of its accomplishment. He arouses powerful loyalty and fierce hatred, for he allows no middle ground and people are either for him enthusiastically or against him with deadly enmity. He probably would fail in holding, or at least in building up, a congregation, for his message tends toward a single theme constantly repeated.

The prophet has a sense of ultimate demand—a feeling of "thus saith the Lord"—and not much patience with men who counsel going slowly. He has no time for the compromisers, while the slower processes of education usually have little appeal for him. He sees clearly the will of God and his task is to proclaim it and demand it now. It is no wonder that the prophetic strain reveals our faith at its best, for without it we would soon have a church with no higher calling than to touch morality with a little emotion. The easiest thing in the world is for the Christian Church to become just a morale builder for whatever society it inhabits.

The priest is something else. He has a settled parish and he serves a particular church. He stays with the people and learns to know them. He baptizes the babies, marries the young people, buries the dead. His families know him in their times of rejoicing and in their hours of sorrow. He has learned to make allowances for weakness and betrayal, and he has developed the patience to believe that his people are a little better today than they were yesterday.

The priest is the servant of the institution, for he sees it as the only way of mediating God's grace to a community. He is concerned with budgets, since the church cannot carry on if it does not pay its bills and support the wider programs. He learns how to work with committees and encourage the janitor to keep things clean, without making him angry. He has to visit from house to house and instruct the children. Compared with the prophet, the priest hews the wood and draws the water.

The priestly function is the practical one of dealing with the small things, which are more important than we think. His is the responsibility of meeting people where they are and patiently trying to bring them grace and power. This is not to say that he ever lowers his standards or substitutes a watered-down humanism for spiritual religion. He does what Paul did in writing to the Corinthians. The famous fifteenth chapter of First Corinthians talks about the mighty hope of immortality and rises to one of the mountain peaks of the Bible in its inspiration. Then immediately, and to our ears rather abruptly, he begins the sixteenth chapter with these words, "Now concerning the collection . . ." Yet the sudden descent from the peak to the valley is more apparent than real, for if it is a religious affair to consider immortality, it is also a holy thing to give to the saints who are in need. But taking the collection is more typically a priestly function.

When the Christian is a priest, he is first of all concerned for the needs of men. The Good Samaritan must bind up the wounds of the victim of the thieves, rather than start an investigation of the cause of crime on the Jericho road. The latter is not unimportant, but the first thing is to save a wounded man from death.

We need the great voices of the modern prophets but unless they are combined with the priestly heart, they are never complete Christians. It has impressed me very much to note how many people have been helped by some deed of kindness which remained with them as the true sign of a man's greatness. It takes a rare kind of man to bring men into the presence of God through his administrative duties. But men are sometimes brought closest to the divine when they work together in the common organizational duties of a church. If the institution of the Church is as central as history clearly proclaims, then the priest is not a man of small importance.

Duke University has a beautiful set of bells in the tower. They were brought from Holland, and I have been told that when they were first set in place they rang almost continuously for several weeks. The central note of a bell can be cast at the foundry, but the overtones which give the bell its unique quality have to be tuned to the terrain, the altitude, the atmosphere of the environment. Which is a parable! We need to have the central note of our lives struck in heaven, but the overtones depend on the local circumstances and experiences of our particular situation. The prophet sounds again and again the central note, while the priest helps us to bring forth the Christian overtones from our trials, our triumphs, our temptations, our defeats, and our victories. Our priesthood is often the human side of our faith.

2.   SPEAKER FOR MEN

If the priest is the servant of God he speaks to men and is sometimes the spokesman *for* men. That is, he mediates the word and the grace to the people and he sometimes puts into words what plain men cannot phrase for themselves. He has sympathy and understanding for the weakness and frailty of humanity.

In our priestly function we are most aware of the need people have for comfort. Christians ought to comfort each other and be centers of encouragement. There is a place for the high and lofty vision of the moral law and the demand of Jesus, "Be ye perfect." But there is also the need for sympathy when the vision has been denied and the world has won its way over us. There is the need for a loving word when sorrow comes to persons and families. There is something to be said for the Catholic Confessional, though there are also some serious legitimate objections to be raised against it. Men need to have a place where they may share their burdens and confess their guilt to a servant of the Lord who is neither easily shocked nor overanxious to judge. This safety is denied to many people in our time, largely because they have drifted away from the fellowship that would provide it. The man who knows at least one other person who will never turn away in disgust nor hurl some righteous denunciation is blessed with one of life's greatest gifts. Christians ought to be such persons to their neighbors, and indeed to any man who needs them.

Forgiveness, as a rule, has to be mediated. We can believe in

God's forgiveness as a theological doctrine, but it is hard for a man to appropriate it personally in a specific situation. Usually God has to find His way into the human experience by way of another person. The forgiveness that comes to me out of a personal relationship leads me to the Throne of God and to that most cleansing of all experiences, the forgiveness of God Himself. This is not something sentimental or unrealistic, but is the beginning of the real healing and the actual reformation.

The modern "peace of mind" school has been rightly criticized for too shallow an approach and too easy a diagnosis. It is often close to charlatanism, while its impossible promises can lead to a disillusionment wherein the man's final condition is worse than his first. Yet the modern Church has so neglected this legitimate need of men for hope and faith that it has prepared the way for those who would exploit human longing for personal prestige. It is so easy to get into a comfortable condition and forget the pain and worry of other people. Men who know the way forget what it means to be lost, and people with the easy gift of making friends do not know how to share the loneliness of the person who cannot seem to establish any meaningful relationships with his brethren. Christians are called on to exhibit a divine concern that will meet men just where they are with the power of the gospel.

Men need not only those who will speak to them in the name of the "God of all comfort," but they need those who can put into words what they would like to say if they were able. The Christian in the role of priest speaks for men. The best example is the pastoral prayer in the service of worship. Here the minister lifts his people to God and expresses for them their needs, their failures, their aspirations, and the source of their help. It is the loss of this understanding that makes pulpit praying one of the most poorly done acts of the modern ministry.

Men long for another world, for they are made with eternity in their hearts. Yet in the noise and struggle of daily living this essential truth about them is often lost, so that they have a terrible sense of something missing and yet have no clear inkling as to what it is. Even successful men begin to wonder why it is that their successes bring them little comfort and small reward. Surely it is an amazing thing that this lost radiance is so hard to trace by a generation that can track down the polio virus and the hidden nature of the atom. But such is the case, which indicates how spiritually blind we have become. The Christian is the one who must hold up this need and this hunger in such a way that men blinded by secular glitter may perceive it.

We have a great hunger for personal status, and for this there is no substitute. It is not enough to receive a large income or to live comfortably. We need to be important to somebody and to some purpose, so that in our own persons we have a significant place to fill and an essential task to perform. It would be nonsense to say that no man has any sense of status unless he is religiously aware, but it is not nonsense to insist that the sense of status which redeems, ennobles, and spurs us on to be our best is a religious experience. There are some of us who might testify that our poor lives have been used by God to bring men into a new sense of their dignity. There are Christians who do this constantly in every company because there is something about them that makes men remember that they, too, are the sons of Abraham.

Men need fellowship with individuals and with groups, which is one of the main contributions of the Church. Sometimes it seems to me that nearly every group understands this truth about men except modern churches. Communists know it and use it to appeal to the unwanted, and the racketeer knows it and builds up his power on the basis of this fundamental human hunger. But the Church, so impressed with business procedure, has neglected the nurture of small groups which meet with the sense of the presence of One who promised to be present wherever two or three gathered together in his name. It is sad to observe how often the Church has the answer if it only knew it. Yet we have made it necessary for alcoholics to find their healing somewhere else, though the most successful method is fellowship and prayer. Because of our neglect there have grown up what Gerald Heard calls *ad hoc* churches, which are really fellowships drawn together by one main need and one great longing. Prophetic religion can so easily lose sight of the significance of this priestly function. Ezekiel, the most priestly of the great prophets, was the one who could say: ". . . and I came to the exiles of Telabib, who dwelt by the river Chebar. And I sat there overwhelmed among them seven days" (Ezek. 3:15).

Some time ago there occurred an unusual incident at a Florida dog-racing track. The mechanical rabbit, which runs about the track as a lure for the dogs, blew up and literally disappeared. The dogs nearly went crazy and exhibited all the signs of a nervous breakdown. The whole purpose of their existence had been destroyed, and the goal they had been pursuing had betrayed them. People sometimes are like that, for too many of the goals they have pursued prove ephemeral. These are desperate experiences for men, who without help circle around frantically. Then is the time for the Christian in his role of priest to bring them to the altar to worship the God who changes not. Then it is vital to grasp the hand of Jesus Christ, who "is the same yesterday and today and for ever" (Hebr. 13:8).

3. GODLY PERCEPTIVENESS

When we begin to think about Christians as a royal priesthood we must give some consideration to the Sacraments, for one of the priest's high functions is their administration. We differ with our Catholic brethren as to the number, and we differ in interpreting their nature and their meaning. But in general we may say that sacraments are outward and visible signs of inward and spiritual reality; and for Protestants they consist of Baptism and the Lord's Supper.

But these two special acts do not exhaust the Christian meaning of this truth. Our religion is definitely sacramental because it is definitely materialistic. That is, it sees in the material things of life the signs of God's presence and His love. The earth is the Lord's, and one of the foundation stones of our outlook on the world is the Old Testament assertion that God made the world and found it good. It is true that certain acts connected with the life of our Lord have certain special powers to become the means of grace for believers. Yet a Christian man cannot go anywhere in the world without being reminded of God's power and love. The world and all its manifestations are symbols of the truth of God in Christ. The Christian as a priest is aware of handling sacred objects every day and as they speak to him of God, he learns how to share that revelation with his brethren.

Men need help in their religion. This is the reason why sacraments are so important in Christianity. There may be a few people who can live constantly in the rarefied atmosphere of high spiritual awareness. But most of us find the other world fading from our consciousness all too often, so that we are in need of having something we can touch or taste or see which will call us back to unseen reality.

It may be that the Catholic Church is wiser in this regard than Protestant Churches. The wayside shrine in Catholic countries serves as a reminder to the traveler that there is One who walks with him and waits for him. The rosary serves to center the mind on prayer, and in a day of much confusion and many conflicting attractions, this is not to be minimized. Regular habits having religious implications carry many a person through difficult times and temptations.

Of course we are afraid of a kind of idolatry which so easily raises the symbols to magical status. That is rightly to be feared, but we should remember that the Jews, with all their hatred of images, had many holy places and many holy feasts which spoke to them of their heritage and their faith. Let us learn to use the signs which can speak to us of Jesus Christ, and especially let us not despise the customs and habits which keep us open to the guidance of the Spirit. The best of these customs is going to church on Sunday.

We cannot minimize the central significance of preaching and the sermon in our Protestant worship. But at the same time we are learning that it is not necessary to make our churches and services as ugly as possible. The trend is in the direction of a beautiful sanctuary and an orderly service, for to be in a place that quiets us and directs our thoughts to God is in itself a helpful experience. Christians ought not to despise anything that encourages men to become conscious of their need and the source of its fulfillment.

Men need help in knowing God when they see Him, and they are ever in need of recognizing a religious experience in the midst of the commonplace. This difficulty is apparent in the New Testament, and our generation, too, looks at divinity and sees only humanity. "Is not this the carpenter's son?" is still the question raised when Jesus passes by. We find it hard to believe that when we feed the hungry we are serving him. Yet this constant awareness is one of the essential signs that we have been with Jesus and learned of him.

Let a man repeat to himself every day the words of an old revival song: "Count your many blessings, name them one by one." It is true that we will be surprised when we consider how much God does for us every day. It is a fine thing to spend a few minutes every night thinking over how many good things have come to us from God. Then as we give Him our thanks, we shall fall asleep with the sense of gifts and care far beyond our deserving. The Christian as priest may not say his beads nor encourage others to do so. But we may be brought close to God if we say our thanks for the many blessings of every day.

There is a good word for us in a letter John Wesley wrote to

Alexander Coates, one of his preachers. Apparently this brother was always stirring up a controversy, and Wesley remarked, "I have preached twenty years in some of Whitefield's Societies, yet to this day I never contradicted him among his own people. I did not think it honest, neither necessary at all. I could preach salvation by faith and leave all controversy untouched." Then he went on with this pointed and frank observation concerning Coates' showing in public controversy. "Indeed you have not a talent for it. You have an honest heart, but not a clear head. Practical religion is your point. . . . O Sander, know the value of peace and love." It is a good word for all of us. For every prophet, Christianity needs many priests who will deal with the practical things of religion, and in the spirit of peace and love, help people find God in the everyday experiences of their lives.

4. GUARDIAN OF THE SACRED

Finally, the Christian in his role of priest is the guardian of the sacred. This sounds somewhat archaic to modern ears, for we have not specialized in setting aside areas of our life as having special value. We have tended to make everything wide open and common; or, to put it in another way, we have been prone to secularize our whole existence.

The Palace at Versailles is a public place now, as any visitor to France finds if he wants to see this home of ancient royalty. But before the Revolution, it was even more available to the public, for the kings had lived without much privacy. It was not unusual for people to roam about the gardens and enter some of the public rooms. Then there came word that a large mob was on its way from Paris, threatening the destruction of the palace and death to the royal family. The guards tried frantically to close the gates but they were rusted, a hundred years of weather having practically soldered them open. Which is a parable! Men can so leave their lives open to every passing climate, that they no longer have left anything inviolable.

This is our modern danger. If a man doubts it, let him remember the things which once shocked him but no longer so much as raise a passing question. Or let him look at the horrible things this generation has accepted which were once regarded as unforgivable atrocities by civilized people. Hitler may be dead, and the evil called communism may be deplored, but the democracies will do well to consider how much these viruses of the spirit have infected us.

The whole stupid scheme of advertising and commercial promotion is to a large extent to blame. On the local level we expose ourselves and our children to television programs which make everything from comedy to fine music a mere means of selling beer and deodorants. When I consider the American children who spend hours before the screens of these contraptions I shudder at what must be happening to their sense of values. We have made business the end and culture the means, which is a complete reversal of values on any spiritual scale. This is a much more serious sign of our sickness than crime or drug addiction. It is reported that after the 1928 debate in the Commons on the Revised Prayer Book, an English M.P. came out muttering that he could not see what the fuss was all about. "Surely," he said, "we all believe in some sort of something."[1]

There are so many things we allow to slip from us, believing that nothing of value has been lost. Take Sabbath observance, for example. In his novel *East River*, Sholem Asch makes the true observation that God gave man the Sabbath so that he could always remember he was a man and not a beast. In the worship of God, man was proclaiming his kinship with the divine. We need not be surprised, therefore, when men who have denied this important part of their heritage feel less and less the need for worship because they have fallen further and further into the animal kingdom. It is not always easy to make a logical case for Sunday observances, but without them life gets earthbound and the soul is dwarfed.

The day ought to be past when a church assumes that by turning its Sunday program into a pious replica of weekly activities it will affect lives. I still get upset when I remember the church that solved its youth program by putting in a juke box and holding a Sunday evening dance. Or we may think we are making progress by setting up a men's group which is a sort of second-rate service club. There is a great need for the Church to see itself anew in the priestly role of guardian of the sacred places of our common life.

One of the hardest sayings in the Gospels is Jesus' word to people who pride themselves on their tolerance: "Enter by the narrow gate; for the gate is wide and the way is easy, that leads to destruction, and those who enter by it are many. For the gate is narrow and the way is hard, that leads to life, and those who find it are few" (Matt. 7:13-14). He may have been an iconoclast, but he was not a humanist. There is in his teaching a clear insistence that without the worship of God there is no real service to men; without reservoirs of inner power and peace there is no changing of men or situations; without the possession of spiritual values beyond price there are no lasting treasures. A man must sell all that he has, if he would possess the Kingdom.

We need to recover our sense of the holiness of God. If we are to suceed in this we must develop the holy habits of prayer, meditation, and the opening of ourselves to the Holy Spirit. It is only possible for us to be transformed by Him if we are willing to take the time and put in the effort to find Him. Otherwise we will do the blasphemous thing so characteristic of our generation, namely, attempt to force our way on God and use Him to attain our own ends. We are in desperate need of the priestly sense of God's succor for the small man caught in a myriad of small traps.

When a man no longer has a holy, sacred, priceless center to his

life he has lost everything. I have yet to meet a man of large accomplishments and exemplary behavior who has not possessed an
inner citadel of power and a personal holy of holies. Salvation for
many a lost and broken spirit is found in the recovery of that inner
integrity. It is the gift of God and it ought to be guarded as man's
most precious possession.

Angelo Patri tells of a childhood incident in school. The alarm
bell sounded which meant a fire drill, and being nearest the door
he went through quickly and was soon out in the yard. The next
day the principal sent for him and, when he was seated in the
office, there came this sudden question: "You were near the big
door yesterday when the alarm rang. Why didn't you hold it open
for the others?" The little boy gulped and explained that he was
going on an errand and, besides, Tim was monitor of the door.
Then the principal said something Patri never forgot. "You knew
the door was to be held open. And you were there. Next time serve
where you are."

It is a good word for all of us. We are prone to center our attention on the big problems, the big opportunities, the big service. But
most of us win or lose in the small situations, the daily routine,
the little testings. The Christian as a priest serves there and channels
the mighty power of God to plain men driven by undramatic duties.
We need the men who can define the great questions and bring
societies face to face with universal issues. But we are much in need
at all times of the man who speaks for men and helps them to see
the universal in the particular. As Owen Wister put it many years
ago: "There's nothing makes this world seem so little evil as to
meet good men in the humbler walks of life." That is the field of
the priests' service.

6
Prophets

WE ARE IN THE HABIT OF SPEAKING ABOUT PROPHETS AS IF THEY were members of a special profession. We see them as pre-eminently citizens of the Jewish nation and confined to a particular period of history, while their modern counterparts are branded as trouble-makers. Our modern division of human affairs into the categories of sacred and secular makes it almost impossible to believe that every Christian ought to be called a prophet. Yet that is one of the names for Christians, and Peter, in his sermon preached to the people marveling at the healing of a lame man, reminded them of their prophetic heritage. "You are the sons of the prophets" (Acts 3:25), he said, and the implication was that they should remember and honor their debt to their fathers.

I would speak of the nature and spirit of the prophetic part of our Christian calling. It is true that some men are called particularly to the prophetic ministry in our time, and every generation has known those great men who have dared to bring the demands of God to bear on every policy and action. It would be a sad day for humanity if these voices were completely silenced or these men ceased to appear. But if we assume that we are excused from ex-ercising this ministry in our lives we have missed the Biblical note. Let us therefore, try to capture something of the spirit, the flavor, the climate of prophecy.

This is one of the great contributions of Hebrew religion. Rather than a priest with a rite and a temple, the wandering tribes of Israel had one who spoke for God. That desert heritage never was quite forgotten, even when they settled in the cities and farmed the land. And, although often they became angry with the prophet and sometimes stoned him, they could not keep from producing him in every generation. For deep in their hearts, the Hebrews could not deny that God spoke to men through men, and it was a terrible thing to hear God's voice and try to silence it. We are the inheritors of that kind of religion and we ought to think of ourselves as prophets.

I. MISCONCEPTIONS AND MISUNDERSTANDINGS

With such a big subject and such a mighty concept, we had better begin by saying a few words about what the prophet is not, for there are many misconceptions in this important field. Then we will be ready for a positive description.

The prophet is not necessarily an eccentric. The greatest of them are not just commonplace individuals either, and there is no use in pretending that mediocrity is the best ground for the raising of prophets. With all this talk about adjustment and normality as ultimate goals, it would be well to remember that Jeremiah was so torn by the strain between his duty and his desire that today he would be considered a man desperately in need of a psychiatrist. I suppose that all the great ones were somewhat neurotic by "peace of mind" standards, and to speak of them as primarily happy men seems to be a shallow judgment. But it is not shallow to think of them as joyful men or as men in harmony with the will of God.

Yet the modern picture of a prophet is a man dressed strangely, having wild ideas and no sense of propriety. The *New Yorker* now and again has cartoons of such fellows carrying signs in Wall Street or on Park Avenue. Some time ago a man dressed in a long robe, with long hair, and carrying a lantern, passed me on the street in front of the Los Angeles City Hall. He carried a sign which read: "I am looking for an honest man." I overheard one man say to another, as this fellow passed us, "This is a good place to be looking for him." Such a person is a prophet in the minds of many moderns. Not necessarily so!

Another misconception regards the prophet as a fortuneteller. One of the preachers of a past generation spoke of Isaiah's putting the telescope of prophecy to his eye and describing events to come some five hundred years in the future. According to this school of thought, God gives some men special knowledge so that they can tell us what the future holds for us. Interestingly enough, this interpretation is more popular today than in the past. Astrology magazines fill the newsstands, and foretelling our futures has become big business. But true religion never sinks to this level and protects us against such exploitation.

The prophet has a sense of history and especially a knowledge of the moral law. He knows that certain causes will bring certain results, so that he can say with assurance that if you do this you will suffer that. He interprets every act from the standpoint of God's will and purpose. Sometimes, as in the case of Jonah, he describes the coming destruction and his prophecy is forestalled by repentance. And sometimes, as it did Jonah, this displeases him. But more often he speaks his word that men may be encouraged to face their situation and be saved.

No real prophet ever announces a precise time schedule, for he remembers that One greater than the Prophets warned against it. The charlatan tries to win his fee by being more precise than an honest man can be. In one town where I lived, a certain group issued a prophecy every December of what the new year would bring forth. But it was such a cleverly written document that almost anything that happened could be read into the vague double talk. The Christian knows a few essential spiritual laws the breaking of which will bring disaster. This he can announce with assurance, but as to the hour or day of judgment, only God knows. There are always too many factors for any one man to grasp.

Another mistaken notion about the prophet is that his message is always negative. We have the idea that when a man denounces men and things he is being prophetic, but if a man speaks in appreciation he is throwing aside the prophet's mantle. Not so. Read that great section of the Old Testament beginning with the fortieth chapter of Isaiah and the gentle words: "Comfort, comfort my people, says your God" (40:1). There is no more healing, encouraging, promising sentence in all literature. Yet let it not be forgotten that it was written by a prophet. The harsh, bitter denunciation which reflects a sort of sadistic delight in picturing the coming destruction of the wicked is not the mark of a Christian prophet. He often has to speak hard truths, but he speaks his truth with love.

Now let us consider a few positive marks of the prophet. I stopped at a railroad crossing a while back and, while waiting for the train to pass, looked again at the familiar sign: "Stop, Look, Listen." It came to me that in a sense this is what the prophet is saying to the people.

He says, Stop! Consider where you are going and where the present path will lead you. Obviously, he would tell us that what we are now doing cannot be continued without paying for it. Instead of blindly rushing forward toward disaster like a lemming, be a man and stop to consider and think. Can you escape the law of the harvest? Will the sowing of wild oats produce healthy grain? Is this what you were made for, and is this what you really want? Stop! Get off this treadmill and find the straight path of life.

Before anything can be done to help us deal with our troubles, we have to stop what we are doing long enough to think through what caused them and where our present path is leading us. It is this unwillingness to stop, or sometimes what seems an inability to stop, that drives us to disaster. We are afraid to consider our ways. Men can be like the herd of swine into which the evil spirit had been sent and, like them, we rush down the slope and into the sea. Stop!

The prophet says, Look! He brings us an eternal measure, so that we may see the daily act in the right framework. So many little things seem big to us if we have no significant reference point, and so many big things are neglected when we live from hour to hour. Israel's prophets did not hesitate to speak in terms of the world, and the great sweep of empires never cowed these citizens of a small nation. It is amazing that such men could see so much from what must have appeared to many as a limited vantage point. Yet their vision encompassed the whole world and they told their neighbors what they saw. When men with such a sweeping view were around, it was impossible to become too local and too parochial. Long before modern wars and modern travel made every man a threat or a blessing to every other man, they could see the whole world and they created visions for limited men.

Can a plain Christian have a vision like that of the Hebrew prophets? The answer is that the plain Christian cannot help having such visions when he sits at the feet of Jesus Christ. For when a man looks into his face, he sees the glory of God. It is this look that makes everything take its proper place and assume its proper size. There are not many men in any generation who can see what is important and what is passing, but Christians are among such men when they remember that they are the sons of the prophets.

The prophet says, Listen! There are too many loud noises that are full of fury, but signify nothing. There are too many loud mouths that send forth big boasts and ridiculous claims, but the voice of truth is not in them. Like that ancient prophet who was called to the mountain that God might speak to him, we discover that His voice is not in the wind, or the earthquake, or the fire. It is as a rule "a still, small voice" and we have to listen for it. We are learning that one of the factors in our nervousness and distress is the inordinate amount of noise in our cities. Listen for His quieting, reassuring, encouraging word.

A part of many services is a call to worship by the choir. Often the words used are:

The Lord is in his holy temple;
let all the earth keep silence before him.
[Hab. 2:20]

It is seldom recognized, however, that these words are from a prophet, and one of the most skeptical ones at that. His was a time of violence and immorality, a time of dishonor and exploitation. All this was true, but "the Lord is in his holy temple." Keep still and listen! For in the midst of all the confusion and turmoil, Habakkuk speaks for patience and waiting. With great honesty and much daring he speaks of God.

I will take my stand to watch,
and station myself on the tower,
and look forth to see what he will say to me,
and what I will answer concerning my complaint.
[2:1]

We admire a man who speaks so forthrightly. Then comes the assurance he seeks, and God says:

For still the vision awaits its time;
it hastens to the end—it will not lie.
If it seem slow, wait for it;
it will surely come, it will not delay.
[2:3]

Listen expectantly, says the prophet, for He will speak to a man and to the nation.

Rebecca West, in *The Meaning of Treason,* writes: "The trouble with man is twofold. He cannot learn truths which are too complicated; he forgets truths which are too simple."[1] Whenever we get away from the prophet's simplicity we try to guide ourselves with complicated reasons for doing what we want to do, though it be immoral. We cannot seem to believe that a complicated age is still amenable to the simple truths announced by the prophets of the eighth century B.C. When the Christian remembers that he is a prophet, such truths are not forgotten.

This is not a matter for only the sophisticated and the wise. As a matter of fact, too much sophistication sometimes confuses men and blinds them to the simple, obvious truths of human life. Thomas Jefferson, in a letter to Peter Carr, written August 10, 1787, referred to the contrast between a farmer and a professor: "State a moral case to a plowman and a professor. The former will decide it as well, and often better than the latter, because he has not been led astray by artificial rules." The prophet is like the plowman, and no matter how murky the atmosphere or how dim the path, after stopping, looking, and listening, he soon has his bearing. Without this profound wisdom, our little cleverness or our impressive knowledge will be in vain.

2.   PERSPECTIVE

The Christian as a prophet is characterized by a sense of perspective, and this is no mean gift. If you see a child drawing a scene you will note that he gets everything out of proportion. The house is bigger than the mountain, while the horse is bigger than the barn. He is unable to make objects assume their proper size in relation to other objects. In this respect, many of us remain children all our lives, and our construction of a plan of life reveals that same distortion to the end. Perhaps a basic weakness in most men's living is an inability or an unwillingness to regard the parts in the light of the whole.

For one thing, we fail to make clear to ourselves what is lasting. We confuse the temporary and passing with the eternal, so that the merely ephemeral receives from us the same treatment as the everlasting. Many a marriage goes wrong right from the start, because young people have put their trust in things that cannot last. It is wonderful to have a pretty wife or a handsome husband. Attractiveness is never an unimportant matter, nor is the quality of style. But the passing years make it plain that the surface qualities are not the essential ones. Many a happy marriage has taken place between rather plain people who have little knowledge or interest in the world of society. It is much more important to marry character than it is to marry beauty, though, of course, the two are not necessarily mutually exclusive. But if the choice is between them, choose character. Sympathy, cheerfulness, unselfishness, and above all, love are the qualities which one had better choose for the long pull.

A small boy went into the lingerie department of a store and shyly confessed that he wanted to buy a slip for his mother, but he did not know the size. The clerk said it would help if he could tell her if his mother was thin or fat, short or tall, "Oh," beamed the little boy, "she is just perfect." So the clerk sent him home with a size 34. A few days later, Mom went back and exchanged it for a 52. But the little boy was seeing his mother in the light of love, and her perfection in his eyes was more important than a perfect figure.

Our amusements are so often deteriorating rather than constructive in their effect on us. We learn to relax by making unreasonable claims on our physical and spiritual reserves. Our recreation ought to re-create and strengthen us rather than weaken us. There are a few places where it is more important to have the right perspective than in choosing the means and methods of our personal recreation.

The number of men who end up in jobs they hate suggests that the first thing to decide is not the immediate salary nor the amount of preparation demanded. I have a friend who is typical of so many men in our time. In his middle forties he discovers that his antipathy to his work makes it almost unbearable. Yet he chose it because it was easy to get into and demanded very little education. Almost immediately, he was receiving a good salary. But if he has seen the whole affair in right perspective, he would have made a different choice twenty-five years ago.

The Christian prophet spots the difference between the temporary and the timeless, so that he does not confuse one with the other. Of course, we have to deal with both realms, but when we confuse them only disaster can be the outcome. When God becomes the central reality in a man's life, he will have protection against the false choice. The sense of eternity will enable a man to look at life from the divine perspective.

Not only is it necessary to be able to see the lasting, it is also essential to recognize the significant. The hysteria of a generation like ours is inevitable when it has lost its faith in God. You are doomed to mistake the unimportant for the important when you are guided by expedient consideration alone. A great deal of the contemporary betrayal of freedom would not have happened if more men had been grounded in the central propositions of the American way. When we despise history we lack the point of view essential to tell the difference between appearance and reality.

Can a man tell the real issues facing America merely by reading the newspaper headlines? Of course not, for they deal not with the significant matters but with the dramatic happenings which so often are in the general field of the scandalous. It is not here that the trends are to be discerned, nor can we learn about the wave of the future from most modern journalism. Read Toynbee, or any thoughtful historian, and he will tell you that on the basis of the real cause of the rise and the fall of societies, the future will probably be shaped by things never mentioned in the papers. The Prophets of Israel were not too much impressed with profits for the ruling class, but they were terribly in earnest about justice and morality. The surface things have changed considerably in the past twenty-eight hundred years, but it is still true that the ultimate things are justice and morality.

Some years ago William Allen White wrote his own story, and it was marked by a most wonderful awareness of the great trends in American life. Yet he was a small-town man, editor of a small-town newspaper. But when you compare his understanding with what is revealed in the stories of many men in far greater positions of prominence you know that it takes more than proximity to great events to understand them or even properly to see them. It takes an awareness of the reality of the unseen.

One of the most distressing things about a church is the way it can fall into petty bickering and quarreling over inconsequential matters. Churches have been split and spoiled by bitter arguments about plans for the new sanctuary, or the dismissing of a dishonest employee, or the appointment of a member to a minor committee. Nothing seems too small to be the cause of strife. Then the Christian prophet must appear to raise the vision above the insignificant to the mighty task of the church. Smallness on the part of minister or laymen will result in small behavior. The best protection for a church in danger of falling into a trap of silly bickering about the inconsequential, is leadership that holds before the congregation the prophetic vision of the Kingdom of God. Church members ought to be led to the place where they are ashamed of becoming involved in the merely passing affair or upset by the merely minor irritation.

When a man has perspective, the daily tasks assume new meanings and the daily loads are lightened. Henry Nelson Wieman put it this way:

If a man could be physically and psychologically forced to do nothing but put one foot successively in front of the other for days at a time, he would either commit suicide, become imbecile, or go insane. But if he made exactly the same movements day after day and week after week under the integrating purpose of walking to the place where he could woo the maiden he loved, or under the purpose of scaling Mount Everest, the process might be an inspiring and immensely enriching experience.[2]

Such is one of the great gifts that the prophetic tradition bestows upon the Christian.

3.   THE PROPER BALANCE

Besides perspective, the prophet has balance. Alfred Webb, son of a friend of William Lloyd Garrison, wrote to one of Garrison's sons to tell him a little anecdote about his father. Once, in Dublin, he had accompanied the great Liberator to a photographer's shop.

> While we waited at the artist's we looked out of the window. It was a stormy day. The wind blew off a man's hat, and he had a stiff race after it, and I remember the shock of my feelings that such a great and good man as your father should remark, that he always enjoyed seeing a man running after his hat.[3]

I do not know of a story about a great man that pleases me more. It shows a fine sense of balance.

Because the nature of life is paradoxical, that is, seeming opposites are held together in tension and unity, it is difficult for men to escape going too far in one direction or another. I once wrote a book called *The Lion and the Lamb*. I still think that the problem of keeping the two together without mutual destruction is a basic problem of life. The coldly logical mind never quite grasps the heart of truth, for there is always a wild, untamed element in it which makes it understandable only to the poet. The poetry of religion gives a deeper understanding and a more assured balance.

Yet theology is one of the best examples of great truths running away into the wilderness of exaggeration, if they are not held in check by their opposites. When you chart the history of theology you are reminded of a sailing ship tacking back and forth into the wind. It does not sail a straight course and after veering far to one side it has to be brought back to the center, but it nearly always goes on past the center to the other side. We do not get great ideas without carrying them too far. The problem is not only false ideas, for any good thing becomes an evil thing when it is cut loose from the anchorage of opposite truth. Luther once expressed this in picturesque language. He compared the world with a drunken peasant trying to get on a horse. Hold him up on this side, and he topples off on the other side. The Christian prophet keeps the balance by holding paradox before us continually.

Extremists are ever in danger of destroying us. Beware of reading only one point of view. Beware of reading only that with which you agree. Let no man make of himself a single party voice. I think there is need for reformers, but such men, except in exceptional cases, can hardly ever keep from developing such a single-track interest that they assume it to be the chief issue facing us. There is a real difference between a reformer and a prophet, and the essence of the difference lies in the width of the base on which they stand. The prophet offers not a panacea but a new mind. His program is nothing less than a surrender of human pride and selfishness to God's will for justice for all men. The Church's devotion to God is not a narrowing thing, but a widening of the human outlook.

The church that is always running after some immediate solution seldom carries the influence of an eternal institution. When we are devoted to seeing and proclaiming the eternal purposes of the Almighty we do not flit from one humanistic answer to another. We are sometimes out of step with the time and we take little comfort from the apparent victories of the day. For only with the balance that comes from a knowledge of the wideness of God's mercy and the all-pervasiveness of His concern can we chart our course and speak our word. The need is for men with the balance to see the whole picture. The need is for Christians who have the prophet's mind and eye.

4. DISCERNMENT OF DETAIL

Finally, the prophet not only has a sense of perspective and balance, he also has a clear perception of details. This is where mere idealists go wrong and it is why *ideal* is a philosophical concept but not a Christian one. The Christian is more of an existentialist. The prophet was never content to state what ought to be done at some future day. He was the voice proclaiming that the immediate step must be taken. That was the source of much of his opposition. Hardly a man would disagree with the long principles, but when it was insisted that something had to be done now, then the prophet was regarded as a troublemaker or worse.

Macaulay spoke a word which applies here:

Many politicians lay it down as a self-evident proposition, that no people ought to be free until they are fit to use their freedom. The maxim is worthy of the fool in the old story who resolved not to go into the water till he had learned to swim.

But sometime one has to start, which usually consists in plunging into a situation without any guarantee of safety or even of success. Delay is the devil's best method and the attitude of waiting for a proper time does more harm to God's plans than any other single item.

The Christian as a prophet is aware that God's will must affect his present situation. It applies Here! Perhaps the best example of this emphasis is Amos. He begins by pronouncing God's judgment on Damascus, Gaza, Tyre, Edom, Ammon, Moab—all neighbors of Israel. No one, I suspect, objected to that kind of preaching, and probably 99 per cent of the congregation agreed with the preacher. But when he turned from this introduction to the body of the sermon, which was a denunciation of the sins of his own people, then trouble began. It always does.

There are enough people singing praises of their own people and of their own nation. Now and again some man will ask why the Christian preacher is so critical of his own country, and the answer is that the more you love a people the more you are concerned that they repent of their sins before it is too late. I think that one can say in all honesty that America has been the most generous nation in history, and it looms head and shoulders over Russia in moral stature. Yet our sins must be pointed out and we must be called to repentance for our hysteria, our immorality, our selfishness. Woe to the nation that has no Christian prophets or refuses to listen to them.

The prophet is a man who can direct the word of God to himself as well as to others. If he cannot himself see himself under God's judgment, he recognizes himself in that position when another points it out to him. Remember Nathan and David. Nathan's greatness was in his confidence that God was no respecter of persons, and if the king was a sinner, the prophet must tell him so. But David also had greatness, which was to see his sin in its true light after the prophet had told his story.

The Christian as a prophet is aware that God is speaking to his own situation, and to his own life. We must stand under the searching light of the particular demands God is making on us. This is a difficult thing to do and it is a rare thing to do it gladly. Not many men have the grace really to look at themselves, but it is this quality that gives a man courage and calmness. One of the things that impresses me most about Christian prophets is their quietness. They are not the boisterous, offensive, mannerless persons so often associated with the self-consciously honest and frank. They are more like Jesus going home to dinner with Zacchaeus and opening up to him his failure and his cure. They tell us what we would like to be if we thought we had the ability and character. Then they tell us how to find the power and what our first step must be. You may be sure that the true prophet is nearly always kind.

Underlying our faith is our belief, founded on experience, that God speaks to men. He may not say always what we want to hear or what we think He ought to say at that particular time. But the prophet, whose hearing has become acute and whose heart is unafraid, will be the saving influence in every situation. Every generation needs him for its health's sake, but our generation needs him for the sake of its survival.

7

Pioneers

As one who knows little Greek and no Hebrew, I have found the modern translations of the Scriptures a very present help in time of trouble. They give new insights as they put the ancient meanings into contemporary terms. This is what Moffatt has done for us in the translation of a word used by Peter in a sermon explaining the healing of a lame man. Although they had killed this One, whom he describes as "the pioneer of life" (Acts 3:15), still it is by his power that men are healed and redeemed. And because Christians are the followers and imitators of Jesus, then it must follow that they are to be a fellowship of pioneers.

It is true, of course, that many times in life we must fight holding actions. There are times when we cannot advance and when our testing comes in terms of hanging on to what we have gained, even when we are weakened by weariness and discouragement. But this is not to be regarded as more than a temporary expedient. This is not the Christian way nor the long strategy of the Church. We are to be on the march, filled with the spirit of the offensive, never content with the defensive position nor the negative spirit. In a word, we are to be the followers of one who was and is the Pioneer of Life.

I.   COLONISTS

One of the famous epitaphs of the West says:

> To Lem S. Frame, who during his life shot 89
> Indians, whom the Lord delivered into his hands,
> and who was looking forward to making up his

hundred before the end of the year, when he fell asleep in Jesus at his house at Hawk's Ferry, March 27, 1843.[1]

This is a rather typical appraisal of too many Christian lives. They are spent in the same worldly, pagan pursuits as their neighbors', but a blanket of sentimental piousness is thrown over them toward the end.

Christians are destined to become something more than people covered over with a thin veneer of religious platitudes. St. Paul says they are to be "a colony of heaven" (Phil. 3:20, Moffatt). You see at once the connection between this insight and Peter's description of Jesus as a pioneer. The pioneer so often is a colonist, establishing in a wilderness or on a frontier a community that is the homeland in miniature.

One of the main marks of the colonist is that he owes his final allegiance to another king. He is a representative of a master who may be far away across the sea or on the other side of a continent. In the final testing, he will be true to his sovereign regardless of the pressures of the immediate vicinity. He lives in a certain locality, but his allegiance is not entirely to the contemporary situation, nor is he content to adjust his customs and habits to those of the local tribe. Unless he remembers whom he represents, he can never be the forerunner of civilization.

Now, this sums up the whole problem of the relation of church and state, which is always an uneasy one for the Christian. He cannot take an extreme position on either side, but must always hold the two loyalties together in a constant tension. He cannot say, for instance, that the state is his maser and he will do whatever it commands under any and all circumstances. The Christian society recognizes that it has no authority to make such a demand, and so it provides the right of men to be excused from its demands when conscience insists. On the other hand, the Christian cannot withdraw from the state and deny its claims. The New Testament is quite clear on this and it reminds all Christians that they are also citizens who owe something to Caesar. Both Jesus and Paul make plain this point, as do the later Epistles.

There is no easy answer. There is a story about a young CO who was brought before a judge during the war. The judge was unsympathetic with the young man's position and asked sternly where he thought he would be if he took such a position in Hitler's Germany. The young man replied that he would probably be in a concentration camp and perhaps killed. "But by the way, judge," said the young man, "where would you be if you were in Hitler's Germany?" Which is to say that the problem is not one facing conscientious objectors only, but it confronts every Christian man. We are a colony of heaven and we owe, therefore, an ultimate loyalty to the King whom the world does not own.

Because we are a colony, we have a home base and a model. We are to build society on the foundation of righteousness and we are to live in this worldly wilderness according to the government of the Kingdom of God. This is why an individual Christian who stays outside the Church is a contradiction. His life must be a proclamation and a demonstration, but the demonstration is a social matter. John Wesley was quite right when he insisted that the Bible knows nothing of solitary religion. Our Faith is ever aware of the community, because it assumes the establishment of colonies of heaven.

There is an old Spanish proverb to the effect that a bird can fly about in all directions, but if it is to fulfill its destiny it must build a nest. The individual Christian may wander about over the earth with spectacular swiftness, making brilliant analyses and prophecies. But the job is done finally only when a Christian community is established in a pagan land, which incarnates the heavenly home and the divine kingdom. In a word, there is a divine necessity for the Church.

2. BUILDERS

Another mark of the pioneer is the building of the means of communication. He is a road-builder. So Isaiah writes:

A voice cries:
"In the wilderness prepare the way of the Lord,
  make straight in the desert a highway for our God."
[40:3]

The great pioneers have all understood the importance of roads, and the most successful conquerors of the wilderness have established the highways connecting the established settlements with the frontiers.

Some years ago we were visiting friends in the south of Wales. One evening our hostess took us for a rather long walk to visit an ancient church in the vicinity. We went across fields, over stiles, and through gates until we found a beautiful old church on a hilltop. I commented that in America we build our churches close to the main arteries of traffic, so they may be seen and are more convenient to attend. The lady took us over to the edge of the churchyard to a wide depression running straight across the fields. "This," she said, "is the old Roman road," and sure enough, the ancient stones were still in their place. When the church was built several centuries before, it had been located by the side of one of those roads the Romans built across Europe and the British Isles. The Romans knew that merely to defeat their enemies was not enough, but to make their victories lasting they had to bind the empire together with roads.

Today we find a different situation in a place like Alaska. It is not necessary to build roads over the difficult terrain of that far northern territory. Instead, airstrips are built, for the airplane is the means of opening up the northland and the new routes are through the air. But the principle is the same. Pioneers build roads on the land, over the sea, or through the air.

The Christian as pioneer is a builder of roads. It is a sign of our Christian failure if we accept the inevitability of two separate worlds with a permanent iron curtain between them. When men accept the future as a long waiting for a war to the death between two mighty enemies, it is no wonder that they lose hope and fall prey to hysteria and fear. The Christian never doubts that under the surface of any ideology there are the sons of God. He believes that what God can do is beyond the measure of man's mind. He is committed to the faith that God wills brotherhood among all men. In the meantime, he must see his vocation as the pioneer who with Christ is dedicated to the task of crossing barriers and preparing the highways through the jungles of hate and suspicion. He is no sentimentalist, nor does he minimize the terrifying difficulties in the way, but he knows that there is no other way to the freedom and opportunity he craves for his children. He has to find the route of communication between enemies. He must find the way of reconciliation.

When Christians see themselves as pioneers they not only build roads, but they also construct bridges across the chasms and rivers separating men. The personnel director of a large corporation, responsible for obtaining the future leaders of the industry has a strange question he throws into the conversation when he interviews a young man. He will say suddenly, "By the way, did you ever want to build a bridge?" If the young man makes no response and seems to assume that the question is stupid, he is dismissed. But if his face lights up and he says, "You know, as a matter of fact, I've always wanted to build a bridge," he is taken on at once. It is in that spirit that Jesus chose his disciples and still calls men today.

The Church brings men together. If there is a church that tests my patience almost to the breaking point, it is the church that is self-consciously for the "best" people only. It is a sickening sight to see a church glory in its exclusiveness and pride itself on its aristocracy and wealth. This is to deny the real nature of the Church. The ecumenical movement in our time is a symbol of an increasing desire on the part of the Church to build bridges again. This "great new fact of our time," as the late Archbishop of Canterbury called it, is symbolizing for us the solution of the real problems of the generation. And if you travel about the world, and become overwhelmed with so much that is wrong, you are lifted up by the witness of the Christian fellowship, which is right. For it is bridging national, racial, and social barriers, and it is the earnest of that universal kingdom wherein dwelleth peace and righteousness.

Chester Bowles, one time ambassador to India, tells of an incident in the life of Gandhi. A young Communist came to see the old man to convert him to a more radical program. He spent an hour with Gandhi but he came out finally, with a sheepish look on his face. "What fools we can be," he said. His friends inquired what had gone wrong. "Nothing," was the reply, "but that little man is the only true revolutionary in our country. We spend ourselves in talking and shouting, and he acts."[2] When Christians become the builders of roads and bridges, the Marxist idea begins to look pretty shallow and inadequate.

3. ADVENTURERS

There has come over our society what can hardly be described as less than a lust for security. We are afraid of communists, or ideas, or change, or controversy, or analysis, or facts. Too many people seem to be saying by their attitudes, "I have made up my mind; do not confuse me with facts." That this change of attitude has come about at the very time of our greatest military strength is interesting, and frightening.

Some years ago my wife and I visited the state capitol in Des Moines, Iowa. Under a large and dramatic picture of the pioneers in the hall was this inscription: "The cowards never started, and the weaklings fell by the way." That is a description of the spirit of the frontier and the kind of men who made the conquest of the West possible. In southwest Colorado, for example, two brothers established Bent's Fort. It was set in the midst of savage and unpredictable tribes of Indians, and it was not far from a hostile Mexico. But the men who operated it preferred the danger and the adventure to the safety of the towns back east. And it was such men as these who won the continent and gave America its heritage.

Dr. Adolph Keller called on me one day. He is one of the pioneers of the ecumenical movement, a respected and beloved theologian and church leader of Europe. In the midst of our discussion, he looked up at a beautiful seascape which hangs on the wall of my office. It shows the waves rolling in and crashing on the rocks of the California shoreline. "That," said he, "is the symbol of America." He added that the mountains, standing mighty, majestic, quiet, are the symbol of Switzerland, but the restless power of the sea is the symbol of America. I wondered if that was as true today as it had been in the past. We want to tie things down and make everything quiet, safe, and dead.

The Christian faith has been an adventurous faith. It has turned old customs upside down. It has sent its lonely spies into enemy territory to tell of a better country and a true King. It has not been afraid of truth and it has preached a divine discontent. It has challenged all the might of the world with a courage rooted in God.

We should not be surprised that this present search for security has sometimes affected the Church. We are prone to think of this institution as an end in itself instead of a means to a greater achievement. It is distressing to find so many churchmen who fear the criticism of the world and assume that to keep their church prosperous and comfortable is the end goal.

During the war a midwestern minister discovered that a Methodist hospital was refusing to take Nisei girls into its nursing school. When questions were raised about this policy, the reply of ministers and laymen on the board of directors was that the hospital must wait to see what the reaction of the community would be. Since the hospital depended on the community for financial support, nothing must be done to jeopardize public opinion. That is a strange attitude for a church to take regarding an obviously Christian policy.

A preacher attacked slot machines in a city where a law against them was being disregarded. He was told that, while they ought to be taken out of the dives, he had better be quiet concerning the machines in the country club, for only the best people played them there.

At least one denomination in our time has hesitated in bringing the United Nations before its people as a subject for discussion, because "it is controversial." When the Church becomes too frightened to consider any subject having to do with the welfare of people and the establishing of peace, it is a far cry from the fearless Christian pioneers who have made it a respected, vital influence in the forward march of civilization. Let the Christian Church pray constantly that she may be "filled with the prophet's scorn of tyranny, and with a Christlike tenderness for the heavy-laden and downtrodden. Bid her cease from seeking her own life, lest she lose it."

One of India's influential figures is Vinoba Bhave, sometimes called the "Walking Saint." As a close follower of Gandhi, he remained very much in the background. But since his leader's death he has become known to millions for his work in encouraging a more equal distribution of land. He walks hundreds of miles each year, visiting villages and urging those who have more land than they need to share a few acres with the landless. He attacks the Communist philosophy and strategy even in its strongholds, and has become the center of a great spiritual movement with the most practical implications. He once said, "If Gandhi had not died, how could I ever have dared to come forward?" One of his friends put it this way: "India needed him. God told him that the time for timidity had passed."[3]

So to the Christians of this generation God is saying that the time for timidity is past. We are to regain the initiative; we are to be adventurers for Jesus Christ.

4.   EXPERIMENTERS

A Russian factory worker heard that his plant was manufacturing baby carriages. He needed one and had no money to purchase it, so he began to filch parts from all the departments of the factory. Later at home he assembled what he had collected. It turned out to be a machine gun instead of a baby carriage. Our world is like that. When we put together what we hoped would make for peace, it turns out to be another instrument to kill and destroy. Our experimentation has not been too successful and we need some experimenters who will try new combinations and different materials.

There has developed in our democratic society an inordinate respect for dead-level conformity. We see it in politics, where the successful politician dreads to be unusual or superior. Has the time come when in our political life Americans prefer the ignorant to the learned, the mediocre to the superior, or the second-rate to the best?

In education, we must serve the masses, which is fine if we do not assume that the masses should set the standard of our life. To a frightening extent, we demand adjustment and conformity on the part of children in the public schools, as if we could no longer find a place for the unusual student. Universities, in the minds of some people, ought to be propaganda factories with no place for controversy or disagreement. The movies now and again try a brave experiment and produce a picture appealing to cultivated tastes, but usually they grind them out for the unelevated desires of the uneducated. Now the liquor people have taken a page from this approach, so that the waitress suggests a cocktail before she takes the order. It is a clever approach, for it establishes the impression that everybody is doing it, and to refuse liquor is to be different.

The Christian is supposed to know "a more excellent way." He believes that "the foolishness of God is wiser than men." If someone insists that the Christian way is impractical, then the obvious answer is that the practical ways we have been using have not worked. Maybe it is time to try experimenting in an endeavor to find spiritual answers to our problems. Maybe we ought to pioneer.

Christians believe in the mighty possibilities of human nature. The power bound up in a man's life is almost immeasurable and, as Thoreau put it, "The man who goes alone can start today." Those who insist that, human nature being what it is, no great change can be expected strike me as being about as sensible as the man who says that because we have always had polio we must expect to have it forever. Dr. Salk did not think so.

Then there are the brethren who are fond of pointing to Christians who are no better than non-Christians. It is usually a matter of comparing Christianity's worst with the world's best. But the real answer was given by C. S. Lewis. He said in effect that Miss Smith, who is a Christian, has a foul temper while Mr. Jones, who is not a Christian and never goes to church, has an even temper. The issue, however, is that you do not know how much worse Miss Smith would be if she were not a Christian, and you do not know how much finer Mr. Jones would be if he were a Christian.

At least I know what Christ did for me, and to that I can bear witness. When I think how far short my life falls from what it ought to be, and what in my best moments I want it to be, it makes me despair. But then there comes to me a picture of what my life would have been without Jesus Christ, and I feel a great rejoicing and thanksgiving for his unspeakable gift. I want to say to every man that until you have tried the experiment of giving him a chance with your life you have merely scratched the surface of your possibilities.

When Professor Nathaniel Micklem of England was in India he observed a poor outcast woman toiling all day in the paddy fields under a hot sun. He asked a missionary what such a person could

understand of the Christian religion. "She understands," was the
reply, "that Christ is stronger than the demons."[4] As he goes on to
point out, she probably had never heard Charles Wesley's hymn:

> He breaks the power of cancelled sin,
> He sets the prisoner free;
> His blood can make the foulest clean;
> His blood availed for me.

But she could understand the experience which those words describe.
Christians have experienced the power of Jesus Christ and they
have faith to follow the One who was the Pioneer of Life wherever
he may lead, and to do whatever he commands. This may not be
the path of safety, but it leads to the most exciting adventure men
ever experience. And it fills us with the assurance that the One to
whom we have given our full allegiance is able to keep what we
have committed unto him, even our immortal souls.

8

Pastors

I HAVE A FRIEND WHO IS ONE OF THE MOST LOYAL AND DEVOTED LAYMEN in the Church. It is always a delight to hear him speak of his pastor, for he uses the word with such respect and affection that one thinks of a relationship more precious than gold. It would be well for us to remember that when the Bible uses the term "shepherd," which is another translation of the word "pastor," it is not usually limited to a particular profession. It has the wide meaning of any Christian in the religious community who knows God and loves his brethren.

The prophets used the term repeatedly, for their thinking is saturated with references to the flock, the herd, the field. Thus Jeremiah speaks of his day as a time when "My people have been lost sheep; their shepherds have led them astray, turning them away on the mountains; from mountain to hill they have gone, they have forgotten their fold" (50:6).

One of the best known and most deeply loved passages in the Bible is the Twenty-third Psalm with its beautiful pastoral imagery:

> The Lord is my shepherd, I shall not want;
> he makes me lie down in green pastures.
> He leads me beside still waters;
> he restores my soul.
> He leads me in paths of righteousness
> for his name's sake.

The New Testament has this same wonderful appreciation for the shepherd imagery. Peter wrote: "And when the chief Shepherd is manifested you will obtain the unfading crown of glory" (1 Pet. 5:4).

In the opening part of the tenth chapter of John, Jesus speaks of his relationship to his followers in terms of the flock and the shepherd:

I am the good shepherd; I know my own and my own know me, as the Father knows me and I know the Father; and I lay down my life for the sheep. And I have other sheep, that are not of this fold; I must bring them also, and they will heed my voice. So there shall be one flock, one shepherd. [10:14-16]

Even such a hurried glance into the Scriptures gives us some sense of the long and hallowed associations of the word "pastor." If this is a name for Christians, it tells us something about our high calling and our status. The word spoken by the bishop to those being ordained elders in my church might well be directed toward every man announcing his decision to be a Christian:

Have always, therefore, in your remembrance how great a treasure is committed to your charge. For they unto whom you are to minister are the sheep of Christ, for whom he gave his life.

Let us consider what it means to be given the name of pastor.

I. SERVING THE FLOCK

The pastor is always deeply concerned for the flock. This concept of service is one of the fundamental ideals of Christianity, which offends a good many people. They have no idea of being servants of other people, especially if they can reap no monetary reward from their service. Jesus insisted that if a man would be great he must serve, and he made his life the example so that none could doubt his meaning. I suppose the word "service" is used more and with less understanding than almost any term in the language. Too often it means that we will serve ourselves with one eye on the main chance.

The Christian in his role of shepherd or pastor is the servant of God, and he puts this first. I recently saw a beautiful film showing an Arizona shepherd taking fifteen hundred sheep on a fifty-day trek from the Salt River Valley to the White Mountains. The owner counted the sheep as they left and counted them on their arrival at the home ranch in the mountains. In spite of the many dangers and seemingly impossible conditions, not one had been lost. The commentator more than once said that this shepherd did not own the sheep and was only working for wages. Yet he risked his life many times to save the sheep; he was on duty twenty-four hours a day, and his own comfort was always the last consideration. Let the Christian as a pastor ponder that man's work, and then look at his own.

We do not own the sheep either, and they are not for our exploitation or profit. We, too, work for wages, and the final accounting will be made one day when we must give an account of those we started with and those we lost. It is a sad day when a Christian forgets that he is a pastor in God's employ.

Many a man excuses his compromises and watered-down witness by claiming that he must serve the people by catering to their lower desires. Too often the vocal parts of the community express a yearning for leaving everything just as it is. Men do not naturally crave the highest, though they are never actually satisfied with anything less. But the first impulse is for ease of conscience, and it often goes hard with the person whose standard is too high. There is always a certain safety in mediocrity.

The Christian pastor may become nothing more than an echo of the less noble aspects of human nature. He may release the tension God keeps on men, and because he is regarded as a spokesman for God his compromise carries authority and disaster. His fault is very great, for he uses his office to betray the One who commissioned him. Our call is from above and our master is God. Our final loyalty belongs to Him, and it is no excuse to say that we are staying with the people. There are times when the Christian as a pastor has to say to his people what God said to the Hebrews through Moses:

"Behold, the Lord your God has set the land before you; go up, take possession . . . do not fear or be dismayed" (Deut. 1:21).

There are few truths more important for the Christian to remember than that he is accountable not to men but to God. When Peter and the Apostles were brought before the Jerusalem Council, their answer was a simple statement of this principle: "We must obey God rather than men" (Acts 5:29). Everything goes wrong with us if we forget this fundamental law of our being, and its neglect explains a great deal concerning the failure of the Church in any generation. Even the secular forces soon lose their respect for religious institutions and leaders who have no loyalty above the desire of the people.

In all of this our example is Jesus. That he was tempted to give the people what they wanted is made clear in the Temptation narrative. To give them bread, or miracles, or conquest would have won an immediate following, but his divinity is nowhere more apparent than in his refusal to make such matters his final consideration. That the temptations were not isolated events is made clear in the Garden, when he prayed for the passing of the cup. It seems quite clear, when we study the life of our Lord, that the clamor of the crowd is usually a temptation. When the going is the hardest, we shall be strengthened if we remember the Man whom the people hated so bitterly for refusing to fit their pattern that they crucified him.

Yet we will be wrong if we assume that our position places us beyond the people. We are not to develop a Messiah complex and assume that our own ideas are always right. As servants of God, we are servants of the people and we do our work not through any superior position, but through our love and by a willingness to identify ourselves with them. We serve the people as if they were the sons of God and not as if they were but thinking animals. It is our task and responsibility as Christians so to interpret their deep desires and longings that they will know their own hearts. We are not so much the Lawgiver on Mount Sinai as the leader of the people through the wilderness.

It is a fine thing when a man or woman brings people together and breaks down all barriers. To such persons will come others with troubles, and those whose hearts are heavy will find in them a source of power. The people will not always receive the counselors' word gladly, but if they are the servants of God and the people, others will never doubt their sincerity. Even the hard word will heal instead of bruise. The early Methodist societies had an understanding of this pastoral function in a marked degree. They considered it the privilege and duty of every Christian to examine one another and comfort each member when he was in trouble. This kind of thing, when undertaken out of indecent curiosity, becomes merely a nosy interference with other people's affairs. But when the motive is the Christian pastor's concern, men are redeemed by that concern.

There is a famous letter written by Cyprian, bishop of Carthage, to his friend Donatus. It was in the year 258, and he was talking about the Christians of that time:

This seems a cheerless world, Donatus, when I view it from this fair garden under the shadow of these vines. But if I climbed some great mountain and looked out over wide lands, you know very well what I would see. Brigands on the high roads, pirates on the seas . . . men murdered. . . . Under all roofs, misery and selfishness. It is really a bad world, Donatus, yet in the midst of it I have found a quiet and holy people. They have discovered a joy which is a thousand times better than any pleasure of this sinful life. They are despised and persecuted, but they care not. They have overcome the world. These people, Donatus, are the Christians.

It is this witness which is so important and it is an emphasis which we sometimes neglect. When the Church shows this quiet joy and harmony, it says more to a warring world than a million sermons. It is the witness of a congregation who proclaim with their lives.

> For he is our God,
> and we are the people of his pasture,
> and the sheep of his hand.

> [Ps. 95:7]

2.   THE SHEPHERD'S GUIDANCE

The Christian as pastor not only cares for the flock, he also guides them. This part of his calling is dependent on knowing the people. It is one of Christianity's basic assumptions that God knows us better than we know ourselves, and so He is our final authority. Jesus speaks of this fundamental characteristic of the shepherd in the Fourth Gospel:

> To him the gatekeeper opens; the sheep hear his voice, and he calls his own sheep by name and leads them out. When he has brought out all his own, he goes before them, and the sheep follow him, for they know his voice. A stranger they will not follow, but they will flee from him, for they do not know the voice of strangers.
>
> [John 10:3-5]

As Christians, we do not take time enough to know our neighbors. Ours is a time of anonymity. In the metropolitan centers people know neither the names nor the conditions of their neighbors living in the same building. It is astounding to discover how few friends people have who live in the big cities and are constantly surrounded by people. But let them need someone who knows them and whom they know, and they find there is no such person. One of our neighbors called on us one evening. He had no other reason than that of welcoming us to the neighborhood. This had not happened before in years. We Americans have become impersonal and isolated.

And the same condition prevails in many a church. Perhaps we have placed too much importance on bigness and too little on fellowship. If there is one glaring weakness in the modern American church, it lies just here. We have much to be proud of and we have a right to take satisfaction in the widespread program we operate. But too often the opportunity and the encouragement for people to meet in small, intimate groups is missing.

In this respect we can learn much from the early Methodist Class Meetings. One of the signs of John Wesley's genius was his way of placing people in groups where they might encourage one another and help one another. It would be foolish to assume that these meetings were always centers of love, for there can be no doubt that some people talked too much and some were too curious about their neighbors' affairs. Yet, in spite of all the obvious weaknesses, such fellowships provided the sense of belonging and sharing. This far offset the weaknesses, and we are wrong when we prefer a comfortable anonymity to a more interfering social setting. For the truth is that when we are in trouble we need the latter.

It is our loneliness that needs healing. We are like Zacchaeus. We have everything our society says we need to be happy, but somehow we are not happy. Remember how that man, who could be a symbol of our generation, waited in a tree to see a strange prophet pass by. How startled he must have been when the man invited himself home to dinner with him. That had not happened in a long time, for Zacchaeus had forfeited the right to have his countrymen accept his hospitality. Nowhere is the sensitive perception of Jesus more apparent than in his understanding that this man needed a guest in his home. It would never have been enough just to visit on the street corner or in the back of the synagogue on the Sabbath. No, he needed to have a friend who would enter his home and talk with him where he lived. And so do many of us!

One of the most promising things happening in our modern church life is the visitation evangelism program which sends men out two by two to call on families in their neighborhood. Not the least value of the experience is what happens to Christians who learn that they have not really fulfilled their calling until they become pastors. For this calling on people outside the church is the first step in entering into the responsibilities and joys of our pastoral name. Strangely enough, this for one man at least was the beginning of freedom, for it set him free from his own prison house of selfish concern. It would be a good thing if once every year each Christian minister should ask each of his members this question: When was the last time you invited another person to become a Christian?

If we know people, we will know life. It is disturbing to learn how little of life many of us really experience. We have too few friends and we move in too limited a circle. At the end of the school year, a teacher was saying good-by to the pupils of her first grade. "Teacher," said one of the little boys, "I sure do like you. I'd like to stay in your room next year, but I've been promoted. Gee, I wish you knew enough to teach me in the second grade."[1] Too many people have that same idea about Christians. They think we might do well enough for the first grade but we are poor guides for people beyond that stage.

We Christians have become sheltered behind a Pharisaic wall and are unable to sympathize with the man who has gone far astray into the wilderness. The average church congregation has all the middle-class virtues, but it often lacks the more important ones of sympathy and loving forgiveness. The substitution of a prissyish goodness for genuine Christian goodwill makes the modern church a refuge for the elder brothers, but leaves no opening for the prodigal son.

Christians ought not to be easily shocked. Read your Bible and learn from the greatest treatise on human nature ever written. There are so many modern "shockers" which are poor, cheap, trivial stuff, compared with that masterly probing of the human heart. The preacher who becomes only the spokesman for the comfortable and the well-to-do has ceased to be a guide to the people. And the lay Christian who prefers a dead respectability to living virtue is no longer worthy of the name pastor. Perhaps the first thing necessary for the Christian who would be a guide to his brethren is to go beyond the careful boundaries of his pride and be at home in the unfenced fields of lawless tragedy.

It is impossible for every Christian to be an expert psychiatrist, nor is it necessary. There are a few fundamental truths which we ought to know, and there are signposts along the way whose directions we can interpret. We know that there is a straight path and there is no

short cut. There is a moral law undergirding all our human enterprise and it cannot be violated for long. There are simple pleasures
which leave no bad aftertaste, and there are immoral profits which
enrich no man. At the end of the day, the man who can live with
himself is wealthy beyond his deserving; but the man with a load of
guilt on his shoulders, bears a burden too heavy for any man to
carry. It is better to give than to get, and in some illogical manner
the more a man shares his best with his brethren the more he has
left for himself.

All this sounds old-fashioned and even archaic, but it is ever new
because it is ever true. The great thing to remember about truth is
that it never grows old and is as fresh and exciting today as it was
a million years ago. We are in great need of people who by their precept and example give us guidance over this well-worn road of experience. The unknown, untraveled road stretches ever before us;
but a generation which assumes that this means the end of tested
principles will soon come to disaster. The road may be new, but the
kind of men who can travel it successfully, and the manner of travel,
are very old and very sure. Let the Christian accept his responsibility
as a guide for the people and as a shepherd of the flock.

Yet we will be wrong if we assume that the man who does not
wander is safe. Charles Kingsley told of a friend who had returned
from tiger hunting in India. He commiserated with Kingsley for
having to live in a small and unimportant village while the world
was so big and the far places were so exciting. But Kingsley replied
to his friend, "It is now some years since I realized that my dwelling-
place must be my prison or my palace. Thank God! He has made it
a palace."[2] The Christian guide will help men when they travel far
afield, but he will also help them see the beauty and the glory in
their own village.

3. THE PROTECTOR'S ROLE

Again, the Christian in his role of pastor is also a protector. From
the winds of fear and hysteria, we are deeply in need of shelter.

Fear in the flock is a terrible thing, and it always brings trouble and death. Even when the path leads along the edge of the precipice, all will be well if no panic invades the flock. Today we know how close to panic we are, for the wildest rumor is frequently accepted as truth, and people seem on the verge of going over the edge at any time. This is a day when our judgment is shaky and we stand ever in danger of destroying ourselves by denying the principles whereby we have lived. Let the Church be our protector in such a time.

What happens to a society is reflected in the lives of individuals. This is a hard time to keep your head, especially if you are young and inexperienced. I am quite sure that young people today are under more severe strain and greater temptation than was the case in my generation. One of my pastors told me not long ago of a young man who came to him all upset because he was about to lose his job. He was sure he was not doing it satisfactorily, and the worry was keeping him from sleeping. When my friend suggested that he take the boss to lunch and tell him about his fear, it seemed too simple and too dangerous. But the pastor pointed out that he had nothing to lose, for he would either be told that he was going to be fired or else he would learn that his fears were unfounded. Well, it turned out that the young man was worried about nothing, for the boss was very pleased with his spirit and performance. How often we need someone outside to show us the obvious and common-sense solution.

Every man stands perilously close to losing his way. Professor James H. Robinson in his fine book, *The Mind in the Making,* said:

> We are all born wholly uncivilized. If a group of infants from the best families of today could be reared by apes they would find themselves with no civilization. How long it would take them and their children to gain what now passes for even a low savage culture, it is impossible to say. The whole arduous task would have to be performed anew, and it might not take place at all.[3]

All of us are in this together, and we are more dependent on each other than we are prone to confess. Many a time it is not because one man is better than another that he escaped making a wreck of his life, but only that he had a protector when he needed him. The older I grow the more I thank God for the men and women who prevented me more times than I like to remember from making an utter fool of myself. The record is bad enough as it is, but it would have been immeasurably worse without the Christian protectors who have been near me all my life.

I have yet to meet a man who has never known the dark night of despair. In those terrifying times, we make the foolish moves from which we do not recover without much suffering for ourselves and for those we love. The path does not always lead through the green pastures, and men without faith find the valley of the shadow their grave. Those are the moments when we need counsel and friendship. Decisions made on the basis of fear and despair, are nearly always wrong. We must wait for a little light to break through or else we must call on someone whose vision is clearer than ours. In these times the Christian acts as the shepherd and becomes the protector.

William E. Gladstone and his wife were a most devoted couple. One of the better known photographs of them shows him addressing an open-air meeting while she stands just behind him holding an umbrella over his head to shelter him from the sun. It is a symbolical picture of many a marriage, and it tells us how often we are sheltered by those who love us. One of our duties as Christians is to become the kind of person who is a protector of people and a shelter for the frightened.

4. LEADERSHIP

Finally, let us note that the pastor is a leader. He knows where the safe valley is, and always he is able to find the way home. The drunk who was afraid to ride on the roof of a double-decker bus because no driver was up there is typical of many of our contemporaries. They have no confidence in the unseen and have been misled too many times by the ones they can see.

The leadership of the Christian as pastor is often the leadership of example and quiet pressure. I have known laymen who seemed to hold no apparent place of leadership in the church, yet they exerted the most potent influence in the congregation. They were leaders by the quiet power of their presence and their spirit. Some suggestions seemed out of order when they were about, and there were some propositions people were ashamed to make because of their nobility. I do not think it is true that a leader is always the chairman or the president of the organization, for such men are sometimes merely the presiding officers, while the tone of the fellowship is determined by men without any official status.

There is a kind of pressure which is evil because it tries to force action toward some selfish goal. Most men will quite rightly resent such pressure, and if it is possible, they will resist it. But the inescapable power of goodness cannot be denied, and a man feels as if he is fighting against God when he tries to oppose it. It is this kind of leadership which the pastor exerts, and there is nothing to compare with it. If we should look at our own lives over the past years we would be surprised to realize how many times we have been better than usual, not because someone commanded it but because someone expected it. That, too, is pastoral work.

Leadership demands authority, but not necessarily an external kind. Much authority is of a very brittle nature because it has nothing except external power behind it. All real authority is of the spirit, and it is accepted by men because they cannot escape the moral rightness of it. I have not forgotten what a colleague of mine said to me shortly after my election to the epicopacy. He said, "You will have only as much authority as you deserve." And it is true. There are few experiences so personally frustrating as to command a man who must obey you and yet to know in your heart that he despises you. The dictator must be the most miserable of men. Jesus Christ on the Cross is still Lord, while Pilate on the throne is still nothing more than a compromising politician.

A man's power and authority are limited by his character. We talk as if this were no longer true, and much is made of the new weapons in the hands of evil men. Of course, it is quite true that certain modern inventions have made it easier for tyrants to rule great numbers of men. Yet I venture to suggest that no system can be operated without the trust of a vast number of people. If a man's only hold on another is that of fear and gain, he will never be safe, for such men are unwilling to risk anything beyond what is absolutely necessary and what is gainful. The advantage is still with men bound together by faith and goodness, and in the long run they will outlast the opposition. Nothing yet discovered is quite so powerful as a man whom his fellows regard as completely dedicated to God and their welfare.

This is no pious, sentimental thing. A minister, seated next to a leading businessman, tried to start a conversation about the soul. After two or three vain attempts, he blurted out, "What do you suppose happens after death?" The businessman, obviously embarrassed, muttered, "I suppose we shall enter into the joy of our Lord, but why bring up such an unpleasant subject?" For many a person, the religious man deals only with unreal, unpleasant affairs. But the Christian pastor is the kind of man whose spirituality is so healthy and winning that he attracts all manner of men by genuine goodwill.

We are in danger of making machinery a substitute for personal quality, and we try to make an institution fill the gap when the spirit of fellowship departs. The only protection we have is that Christians who are also church members shall not forget their pastoral functions. The legend says that the devil walked down the street one day with a friend. They noticed a man ahead bending over to pick up an object. The friend asked, "What did that man pick up?" The devil replied, "A piece of the Truth." "That is bad business for you," said the friend. But the devil answered, "Not at all. I am going to let him organize it."[4] Have you noticed how truth loses its appeal and its power when it gets organized? Do you observe that the Church loses its influence when it stands in the world as a mighty machine rather than a marching army? Christians must never neglect or minimize their pastoral responsibilty, and the laity must remember that one of the names for Christians is pastor.

9
Perfectionists

However much we may speak about the practicality of jesus' way of life, one verse seems to be the impossible counsel of an impractical dreamer. It is, "You, therefore, must be perfect, as your heavenly Father is perfect." (Matt. 5:48). Does he not know that to demand such a standard will at once alienate most men from him? Whatever else we may think about our possibilities we do not assume that we can be like God. It may be that our generation finds these words more repelling than some others, for we are terribly aware of the depths of sin. The optimism of the beginning of this century might have been able to accept such advice, but not the pessimism of its latter years. If Jesus meant to shock us out of our complacency, he has certainly succeeded.

The bishop in the Methodist Church asks nineteen questions, first formulated by John Wesley, of every young minister seeking admission into one of our Conferences. The second question is, "Are you going on to perfection?" and the third one asks, "Do you expect to be made perfect in love in this life?" The boys stutter when they answer these, and I have yet to see anyone reply glibly or thoughtlessly. There have been several times when young men have come to see me personally before answering these questions in public, and we have had to discuss together just what is implied. I sympathize with those who find them difficult and I honor those who, taking them seriously, want it clearly understood what they are not promising.

The truth is that any hint that we are expecting perfection in this life seems like boasting. Wesley's doctrine of Christian Perfection is one of the most neglected teachings of modern Methodism. We are somewhat embarrassed even to confess that we are aiming for perfection, for this sounds too presumptuous for ordinary mortals. Our whole attitude leads us away from such thoughts.

There was a choir director in one of the churches I served, who hardly ever went through a service without one or more blunders. If the choir managed to get through the anthem without a noticeable mistake, then he would come in at a wrong time with a response. One morning he decided to sing the last verse of a hymn without the organ, but the organist did not understand him and neither did the congregation. The result was far from a happy one. When I objected, his answer was, "One mistake in a service is nothing to complain about. What are you—a perfectionist?" And the answer was, "Yes." So far as a morning worship service is concerned, anything less than perfection is not to be endured.

We have developed an inordinate love for amateurs and amateur performances. I have heard enough about how much good the amateur play does for the actors and too little about the pain such bungling dramas bring to the audience. There may be a place for the usual Sunday-school pageant, but it is a place where I try my best not to be. We have been content with such low standards in our church activities that no one expects much and very few attend except the parents and close friends of the participants.

Why should it be considered an uncomplimentary designation to refer to a man as a professional? A professional is a man who believes that what he is doing ought to be as near perfection as he can make it. We have excused second-rate performances rather than demand first-rate ones, and all in the name of some special advantage the amateur is supposed to have over the professional. If a thing is important at all, or if it is worth spending any time on, then give me the professional every time.

Now we expect perfection from machines. An automobile capable of only an "amateur" performance is soon discarded. The airplane has to be perfect. Our machine age demands machine tools that can be exact to the one-thousandth of an inch. Yet in human affairs we are still content with the bungling inefficiency of the Stone Age, and in our own human achievements we consider it bad manners to challenge behavior with too high a standard. The professional football team aims for the smooth and polished perfection of a machine, but the men's organization in the church can be as useless as a prairie schooner on a freeway.

I wonder if some such consideration was in the mind of Jesus when he demanded of his followers nothing less than perfection as a goal. Over against the compromising standards of the past, he called for a new people who would be content only to accept the standards of God. We are not to be fashioned by the world's ideas in this matter, but to keep ever before our vision the perfect nature of God. At least we can be sure that a man becomes no bigger than the best he has accepted. If we smile at the impossible aims of the past, let us weep at the little aims of the present. For Christians, the demand is perfection, and whatever we may accomplish or fail to accomplish in the world, we are expected to keep this standard before us. At least one thing is certain: if Jesus had said, "Just do the best you can under the circumstances," we would not have remembered him. His demand for perfection haunts us forever and it makes him unforgettable.

Baron von Hügel once told Rufus Jones, that for a person to be canonized as a saint in the Roman Catholic Church he must fulfill four requirements. First, he must have been loyal to the Faith of the Church; second, he must have been heroic; third, he must have been the recipient of power beyond ordinary human capacity; fourth, he must have been radiant. This is the kind of Christian perfection that John Wesley would approve, and it is the only kind of Christian saint who can change the world. Let these four qualities form our outline as we consider the Christian as a perfectionist.

1. LOYALTY TO THE CHURCH

First of all, the Christian perfectionist will be loyal to the faith of the Church. This means something different for a Protestant than it does for a Roman Catholic, and we had best point out these differences at the beginning. We are not advocating here that the Christian simply says yes to all the demands of an authoritarian church. This is too easy and far from the deep meaning of loyalty. It falls into the same category as saying, "My country, right or wrong." No institution is always right, and just because men are placed in high positions of authority in the Church does not mean that they are saved automatically from error. There have been times in history when the Church has stood as the chief barrier to the accomplishment of its own true aim.

Yet the Church is not an option, but a necessity, and it is of God. Within its fellowship there have been preserved the Christian treasures of all the years, and it has been the rock on which Christendom is founded. The man who despises it is cut off from the Kingdom by pride. The man who seeks its destruction is an enemy of our Lord, who loved the Church and died for it. The man who seeks to bring strife among its members wounds the body of Jesus Christ. Whatever word of criticism a man feels he must speak against the Church must be spoken in love and with self-identification.

Nor are we speaking of an unquestioned acceptance of a static creed. We shall not imply that creeds are unimportant or unnecessary, yet it is important to recognize that "the written code kills, but the Spirit gives life" (II Cor. 3:6). God will not be reduced to formulas, equations, or creeds, though such matters may be of some service in pointing directions. We can be helped by reading how other Christians have phrased their experience, but we should always keep in mind that experience is never precisely the same for any two persons, nor is it ever completely amenable to verbal boundaries. One of the most shameful things I know is a poor literalist, who tries to put a creedal silencer on one of the authentic, prophetic voices of the Church.

Loyalty to the faith means great expectancy. This is illustrated by Pastor John Robinson, who told his congregation as they departed for the New World that there was more light yet to break forth from the Scriptures. Whenever a man seeks to make of Christianity a closed and finished system he betrays his lack of understanding. The Church's faith is not pointed backward, nor is its only contemporary significance a recapture of the past. Rather it is a faith in the God of the living, and a promise of a Kingdom not yet fully realized.

Loyalty to the Church means submitting our private opinion to the judgment of the saints. The adamant individual who will not have his opinions tempered by the Tradition is too proud and too rigid to find the truth. The man who indicates that the pacifist or the opposer of loyalty oaths is automatically unchristian is himself the incarnation of betrayal. For we shall have differing ideas about these matters, but the witness of the Church is that men may differ and still be loyal and respectful of one another and the institution.

We have had churchmen who have put their economic theories above their religion, and then without any understanding of their blasphemy have blandly announced that they are capitalists, or free-enterprisers, or legionaires first and Christians second. Let it be understood clearly that God will not be content with the second place in any man's philosophy. The shameful attacks that have been made on individual Christians by their brethren in the name of some superpatriotism is one of the most flagrant betrayals of our allegiance to the faith of the Church.

The Church believes in men as the sons of God, and this provides no place for the blackening of character or the smearing of reputations. It believes in the supremacy of conscience, so that even if we disagree with others we must respect them if they are honest. The Church has had long experience in many countries and under many regimes. We had best respect that wisdom and that seemingly out-of-date point of view. Above all, the Church is the greatest and most inclusive fellowship in all the world. When we preserve it we serve the present age; and when we weaken it we bring harm to all people. None of this means mere acquiescence, but rather a positive, critical loyalty.

Ignatius Loyola in his *Spiritual Exercises,* intended for the training of Jesuits, says that "we ought always to be ready to believe that what seems to us white is black, if the hierarchical Church so defines it." That to a Protestant is errant nonsense and a complete denial of man's dignity. But to quote H. R. L. Sheppard:

> There is indeed a sense in which the Church—"the whole congregation of faithful people dispersed throughout the world," to use the charitable definition of the Bidding Prayer—may yet be spoken of as it was many years ago by the author of *Ecce Homo* (a book that still abundantly repays attention), as "the moral university of the world, not merely the greatest but the only great school of virtue existing."

The saint is close enough to perfection to understand this truth, and he gladly gives his loyalty to the faith of such a fellowship.

2.   CHRISTIAN HEROISM

In the second place, the saint approaching perfection is heroic. This is one of the Christian qualities we minimize, and so we fail to get a true picture of what Jesus demands of his followers. For instance, when was the last time you heard a sermon preached on the text: "Blessed are those who are persecuted for righteousness' sake, for theirs is the kingdom of heaven" (Matt. 5:10)? We can hardly believe that there is blessedness or joy or happiness in persecution, and a generation that prefers to hear about peace of mind will hardly welcome a sermon on Christ's demand for heroism.

We have missed the clear insight of Jesus that there is a close connection between courage and happiness. The coward is never happy. Unless a man stands for something, he cannot respect himself nor can he know quietness of mind and conscience. The men who keep their eyes only on the expedient matter and the personal advantage do not end up very well. But if you know a man who has been true to his convictions, even when they cost him much, you know a man whose inner joy makes all the trivial successes cheap and unsatisfactory.

We will do well in these days to remember the words of Emerson: "God will not have his works made manifest by cowards." Such has never been His way. The Bible is the story of heroism, and the early Church won its victory because it was full of brave people. The rugged Puritans have come in for much criticism in our time, but no one has ever questioned their bravery. They had "an answerable courage" which provided America with one of its most precious heritages. There have been times when it took stamina to identify oneself with the Church, and it has always been true that men who made the Church relevant were men of great courage.

No one can doubt now that we live in a tough world. If it seemed at one time that civilization had sailed into a safe harbor, that illusion is dispelled and we know that we are in for difficult days for as far ahead as we can see. The revolutions now flaming across the world, and especially in Asia, are not gentle affairs. Witness the Mau Mau uprisings in Africa, and read such a novel as *Something of Value*. Here is revealed a rushing cruelty and bitterness that seems to deny any sign of civilized culture. We are back in the time of darkest savagery and we learn that just under the surface veneer there is a wild, untamed brutality. Does it seem that a compromising, easygoing, well-meaning attitude will have any chance against this kind of movement? It is obvious that over against the fierceness of a subjugated people's revenge there must be set a heroic faith.

Or look at the Communist threat to our world. Whatever else we may say about this spreading tyranny, no one doubts but that it is a tough movement. We are put to shame when we observe what people sacrifice for communism and then note what Christians are willing to do for their church. In all parts of the world we are learning again that when people believe something with all their hearts they have power and they win converts. Nothing takes the place of religion, and when communism becomes a religion, then its only answer is a devoted army of the Lord.

To make this clear, I want to quote from Whittaker Chambers' odyssey, *Witness*:

When I was a Communist, I had three heroes. One was a Russian. One was a Pole. One was a German Jew.

The Pole was Felix Djerjinsky. He was ascetic, highly sensitive, intelligent. He was a Communist. After the Russian Revolution, he became head of the Tcheka and organizer of the Red Terror. As a young man, Djerjinsky had been a political prisoner in the Paviak Prison in Warsaw. There he insisted on being given the task of cleaning the latrines of the other prisoners. For he held that the most developed member of any community must take upon himself the lowliest tasks as an example to those who are less developed. That is one thing that it meant to be a Communist.

The German Jew was Eugen Levine. He was a Communist. During the Bavarian Soviet Republic in 1919, Levine was the organizer of the Workers and Soldiers Soviets. When the Bavarian Soviet Republic was crushed, Levine was captured and court-martialed. The court-martial told him: "You are under sentence of death." Levine answered: "We Communists are always under the sentence of death." That is another thing that it meant to be a Communist.

The Russian was not a Communist. He was a pre-Communist revolutionist named Kalyaev. (I should have said Sazonov.) He was arrested for a minor part in the assassination of the Tsarist prime minister, von Plehve. He was sent into Siberian exile to one of the worst prison camps, where the political prisoners were flogged. Kalyaev sought some way to protest this outrage to the world. The means were few, but at last he found a way. In protest against the flogging of other men, Kalyaev drenched himself with kerosene, set himself on fire and burned himself to death. That also is what it means to be a witness.[2]

Does this frighten you a little bit? It frightens me a great deal, for I do not know whether that same heroism would be manifested in defense of my faith. I do not know how many Christians are ready to stand heroically for Christ. We have never lacked for martyrs in the first century or in the twentieth, but is the general level of our devotion high enough? Can we kindle the imagination of the non-Christian world by the witness of Christians? I do not know.

Everyone is in favor of a spiritual awakening, according to the speeches one hears in churches, lodges, service clubs, and even in political meetings. This has become well-nigh a standard approach, whether we are talking to the NAM or to the labor unions. Yet there seems little willingness to define just what is meant by such an awakening, and there is no attempt to state the conditions for such an awakening. Will it come about by talking about it? No! Can it be produced by people who only earnestly wish for it? No! Is it to be had on any effortless basis? Of course not!

What will we pay personally for a spiritual awakening? That is the real question. We will have to reorder our lives. It means taking time to explore the spiritual laws and then practicing them. It means sacrificing some of our profits and our comforts for more justice. It means becoming men of character who will unselfishly give of our time and money to lift the moral tone of the community. It demands a concern for men who can never repay us for anything we do for them. Do we still want a spiritual awakening or are we just talking about something we have no intention of seeking?

The world will not be changed except as we are changed personally. The trouble with the world is the trouble with me, and on the basis of my own big pretensions and small practices it is a wonder that things are not worse than they are. It is so much easier to advocate sweeping reforms to be brought in by legislation or organized pressure groups. But such methods accomplish little that is lasting or deep. Until we strive heroically for a Christian perfection, we shall not have the spiritual awakening in time to save us.

As Martin Luther walked into the presence of Charles V to answer the charge of heresy and possibly to give up his life, an old knight said to him, "Little monk, I like the step you take, but neither I nor any of our battle commanders would take it." The men who have made the Church great have been brave men. We are to aim at perfection, which demands that we find that reservoir of courage God provides for those committed to going all the way with Him.

3. POWER FROM BEYOND

The third mark of the man going on to perfection is the possession of power beyond ordinary human capacities. It is the exhibition of spiritual might and the wielding of the weapons of faith. It is facing tasks regarded as almost impossible, humanly speaking, and achieving their accomplishment in the name of Jesus Christ.

One of our greatest weaknesses as Christians is a willingness to settle for too little. We are afraid to trust the unseen forces promised us and so we are constantly adjusting our future plans to our present observable resources. When we remember the courage shown by the early Christians with what must have seemed such limited power we cannot be very content with what we are doing in comparison. For the base we operate from is so much broader that one would expect much greater scope in our enterprise.

Perhaps nowhere is it clearer that our confidence is in the material realm and not in the spiritual promises of the Scriptures. We build our churches on the basis of financial limits set by past experience. Too often we adjust what ought to be done to what can be conveniently done. Now and again a group of Christians will launch forth on a task so magnificient that we regard them as foolish and impractical. When they succeed in carrying through to completion what they have begun, we search for explanations anywhere except in the realm of faith.

In our own lives we betray the same doubts about our spiritual resources. We act as if God were not, and indeed many a man implies that since the discovery of atomic power things are out of hand for the Almighty. We trust the power of science to do our will, but we have so little confidence in God's redeeming might. It is no wonder that we fail to impress a generation which needs a saving word of hope.

The great discovery of religious men has always been the power of God. Moses was changed from an ordinary shepherd into the founder of a nation and the lawgiver of the world when God convinced him that He was able. Pentecost, by revealing the irresistible and dependable power of God, changed a fearful group into a church that became like a mighty army. We are so determined to be theologically correct that we are afraid of the exuberant enthusiasm of men who believe one thing with all their hearts, namely, God is Power.

It has become the custom to smile in a superior fashion at the past generation which dared to talk about the world for Christ in one lifetime. It did not happen, but are we sure that it could not happen? Who knows what a generation of devoted Christians might accomplish if they believed in God's power? At any rate, I take my stand with those who dare to believe that all things are possible with God, rather than with the fearful Christians who show no more faith or evidence of adequate resources than their pagan neighbors.

A professor in a small church college once made this appraisal of himself and his faculty colleagues. "We don't drink," he said. "We don't swear. We don't smoke. We don't dance. We don't play cards. But we have no important virtues."[3] Ah, yes! We have left undone those things we ought to have done, chiefly the demonstration of power from above. If we were willing to become perfectionists to the extent of letting God pour into us all the power we could contain, then sinners would be converted and the whole climate of our contemporary life would change.

4. A SAINTLY RADIANCE

Finally, a saint is radiant. It is this quality which is so often lacking in modern churchmen. We have plenty of good, solid people who are the salt of the earth, but we are in desperate need of the kind of goodness which is full of sparkle and excitement. The idea of dullness and the idea of religion have become so intertwined that when one comes to mind the other is never far from our thoughts. We can expect radiance from movie actresses, but we do not expect it from Sunday-school teachers. Television characters are expected to exude a kind of phony enthusiasm as a part of their job, but laymen and preachers are so often negative when they refer to their religion.

There was a woman who wanted to get her neighbor's opinion about another woman without committing herself. When she inquired about her, her neighbor replied hesitantly: "Well, at least she is a good woman." Whereupon the other answered eagerly, "I don't like her either." Thus do we interpret goodness. It is little wonder that the world so often passes by the Church when it is seeking relaxation or stimulation.

In Jesus' time, the Pharisee was considered to be a pious, orthodox, good man. He made his piety a heavy burden and with a sad countenance in order to impress the people he stood about on street corners. He did not fit in with our Lord's idea of the good life. Jesus ridiculed such behavior, and by his own example made it clear that his followers were expected to have a joyous time. He went so far that his enemies called him a winebibber and a glutton. He was as welcome at a wedding as at a funeral; he was at home with children and with their grandparents; he regarded goodness as a great adventure. The Scriptures even speak of God laughing.

The Christian needs to be a kindling man, which is to say he must have an inner radiance. This is something quite different than a professional sales technique which some men put on as their wives put on make-up. It is the quality of inner joy and a sense of being involved in the greatest of dramas. It is the assurance that history and human destiny are ultimately in the hands of God. It comes from a living faith and a knowledge of victory. He must do whatever is necessary to keep life from tarnishing him with dullness.

Somehow, he must learn how to let God show him the daily miracles and the constant marvels in the world. This renewal of the freshness of our life is the fruit of an adequate, healthy devotional life.

Congregations ought to be centers of radiance. It cannot be created by manipulation, although there are certain material aids. Let the sanctuary be cheerful and let the service march. Let provision be made for the welcoming of the stranger. But, most of all, let the worshipers come expectantly, for in that attitude of mind God will certainly be present. To such a church, young people will be drawn and children will feel at home there. It is the high task of the Church to open our eyes to the glories we ordinarily pass by and to remind us of God's watchful care over us every moment.

One of the most precious gifts God gives us through Christ is radiance. I heard a strict Calvinist marvel that people could sing John Newton's great hymn, "Amazing Grace." For me, the case is just the opposite. I marvel that any Christian cannot sing it. For unless our life is completely different from others', then our whole being is a testimony to the amazing grace of God that saved such wretches. Is it really different with others? Is there any man who can keep from crying out with joy when he considers all that he owes to Christ? Can any man doubt God's providence when he considers all that might have happened, and was prevented? What man among us is able to be dark and gloomy when there is manifested continuously the power and grace of God?

Let us consider again that the gospel means "good news." Jesus told many a parable which pointed up the joy that comes to one who has found the Kingdom of God. It is like finding a treasure in a field, or a pearl of great price, or a lost coin, or a lost son. The same spirit invaded the darkest experiences of Christians through the years. It is quite astounding to note that the testimony of so many outsiders speaks of the strange peace and joy that Christians have possessed.

In more recent times, material welfare has been substituted for spiritual joy. Happiness, we have assumed, depends on what we own and what we control. It has been science, not theology, to which we have turned for solace and contentment. Yet with all the artificial light and brilliance we can produce, radiance such as the saint possesses passes us by. This quality is one of the most needed possessions of our day, and I believe it is the gift of Jesus Christ. We shall not secure it from any worldly source, though we continue to seek it there. Only God can set our hearts and minds alight.

When William James died, Mrs. James asked Dr. George A. Gordon to conduct the funeral service. She wrote to him: "I want you to officiate at the funeral as one of William's friends, and also as a man of faith. That is what he was. I want no hesitation or diluted utterances at William's funeral."[4] We have had enough of the hesitations and the diluted utterances. We are in need of radiant men and women whose faith sets their hearts aglow with hope and joy. Christians are to be satisfied with nothing less than perfection, for that pursuit makes them saints, always to their great surprise.

III

DEMANDS

10

To Become

SOME TIME AGO, IN THE SAN FERNANDO VALLEY, A GROUND-BREAKING ceremony for a new building was held. But the time-honored procedure for such an event was rudely changed. There were no prominent citizens to make speeches and there was not a shovel in sight. An animal trainer had been invited to bring along one of his charges and, at a given signal, the animal began to dig. Probably for the first time in history, the ground was broken for a new building by a gopher.

Now, it may be that I am making too much of this, and you may say simply that this is the kind of thing you might expect in Southern California. I believe, however, there is something symbolical in it, and just a bit frightening. It seems to say that we are no longer willing to proclaim purposes for our new enterprises, and we will not commit ourselves to high-sounding aims. No, we will sink back to the animal level and let a soulless gopher be the sign of our plan.

Everyone seems to feel capable of analyzing our contemporary situation and to proclaim what is wrong. The solutions may vary considerably, and most of them are partial, made on the basis of prejudice rather than fact. But everyone knows things are wrong and is certain that his way will set them right. Let another join the chorus and prescribe a cure—or at least let him comment on the disease.

The most astounding thing about this generation, to me, is its tremendous power and its tremendous fear. One can understand the fear of a nation that is weak, but how do you explain the fear of a nation that is strong? On the one hand, we have more external control over our destiny than any generation before us and, on the other hand, we are so pitifully uncertain and faltering in charting our course. We have developed a desire for security so overpowering that we will vote any budget if it is even remotely connected with security. One of my friends, who heads the personnel department of a large industrial concern, tells me that young men often ask two questions right at the beginning of the interview: (1) What are your retirement provisions? (2) How about vacations and sick leave?

The rugged faith in ourselves which characterized Americans in the growing days of the Republic seems to have deserted us. We make speeches about our way of life, but in actual practice we assume than any Communist is so dangerous that if a man is seen in his presence we cast suspicion on his future trustworthiness. We do not act like a confident people. It is the easiest thing in the world to start a panic or arouse hysteria. People in this mood are not prepared for leadership, and we should not be surprised when other nations question our maturity. Yet, since we must lead whether we like it or not, it is of the utmost importance for the whole world that we manifest confidence and faith.

But how do we find faith and where is the source of confidence? There is only a religious answer to this question, and a generation that will not accept religion will search in vain. For faith is from God, and confidence is spiritual in its nature. These are not products of our making and they are not produced by our cleverness. They are the gifts of God and are bestowed on men who are humble enough to subordinate all their achievements before this ultimate need. Power to keep things in hand and maintain some control over destiny are in the hands of the One in whom we live and move and have our being. The chasm between our possibilities and our actual achievements can be crossed only over the bridge of faith.

When King Darius came to the den of lions in which he had

put Daniel, he was seeking the answer to a question. He had not slept much, for he had been caught in a legality and he had no desire to destroy Daniel. His question was not directed to Daniel's ability to survive, but to the power of Daniel's God. It was not in the man himself that he hoped, but in the man's faith: "O Daniel, servant of the living God, has your God, whom you serve continually, been able to deliver you from the lions?" (Dan. 6:20). The question about a man centers not so much in his own power, but in the power of the God he serves.

If we can find the way to faith in the power of God we can be saved. He is abundantly able if we only believe. John makes clear this truth about Christ when he says that "to all who received him, who believed in his name, he gave power to become . . ." What a heartening word is this for our time! If we can accept this affirmation of faith, we will come out all right. This is Good News indeed, for the power to become children of God is more important than hydrogen bombs. Let us consider this "power to become."

I.   CAPTURED BY A DREAM

For one thing, Christ gives us the power to become captured by a dream. One of the marks of a Christian people is that they are wide open to spiritual promptings and moral urgings. America's greatness lies in this realm. Waldo Frank, in *The Rediscovery of America*, puts it like this:

For our hope, there is the truth that we are a capturable people. It is in our blood to be captured; to be captured "high." Among the colonials were men who had been won by the "new" ideas of Europe; Puritan, Calvinist, Quaker, etc., were capturable men beyond their conservative brothers. . . . Often have the Americans been captured; and never remain captive! . . . Aristocracies captured the colonials, captured the Revolution (turning out the true settlers who were tories); libertarians and romantics captured the young Republic; countless sects and panaceas have for a day won fragments of this capturable people, who never remain settled. We are still volatile; still, hence, dissatisfied; still capturable. What will happen if there come a group or groups of men to capture this longing folk . . . a group who have really, what they claim to have, and what the folk need?[1]

Now, this may be the chief characteristic of a truly hopeful people. It may be the most dependable sign of young people who have a faith to live by. Perhaps a tired old nation is no longer capturable by a great idea or a big hope. There comes finally over a society a kind of disillusionment with every idea of progress or improvement. The prophet speaks in vain and the dreamer is regarded as a fool. Every great revolutionary movement depends on this quality in people, and its success can be measured by its ability to arouse men to high endeavor again.

Men can be so beaten down that the ability to grasp a new hope is well-nigh lost. Edwin Markham was talking about such a one in his poem, *Man with a Hoe*. Such creatures have been something less than men, and this is their tragedy. It is also the judgment upon processes which have made them so. Men with the divine spark still alive and with some awareness of their divine sonship cannot help responding to the best when they see it. The world weariness which comes to the worldling never has its way with the religious person. For, no matter how hard the road and how many times defeat has been encountered, at the center of man's being there is this everlasting *Yes*. To be human means to be capturable by a dream.

This has its dangerous side, as our generation has learned. Men not only can yield themselves to the good cause and to the great crusade, but they can also give themselves to the evil promises of bad men. Witness Germany and Hitler; witness China and Mao. The evil genius can set a trap for the unwary so that white seems black and evil seems desirable. One of the things that strikes the outside observer of these mad floods of hatred and destruction is that many a man who yielded to them is unable to explain why afterwards. It all looked so different at the time and, until the debacle, it even seemed justifiable. There was seldom a deliberate choosing of the wrong, nor did most men consciously turn their backs on decency.

This means that to be human is to be in danger. There is no final safety for any man or any society. Men, being what they are, can be captured, indeed they must be captured by something; and when that something is betrayal, how great is the disaster! There are men who purpose to seduce the public, and their opportunities have seldom been greater than just now. For they have the instruments for mass appeal and they have learned the clever techniques of deceiving the masses. They make their appeals to the unthinking, the uncritical, the unethical. Unfortunately we have more of such people than is healthy for us. With all our cynicism and so-called hardheadedness, confidence men still make a good living and shoddy products are still sold. Cinderella remains our favorite story, and winning a fortune on a TV quiz program is still our idea of success. This incurably romantic quality in the heart of man makes him a victim of those who would capture him for their own profit and his destruction.

But the bright side of this picture far outshines the dark shadows. A friend of mine, Virgil Kraft, wrote some lines well worth quoting:

> Spring shows
> what God can do
> with a drab and dirty world.
> Deep in the heart of all things good
> is the urge to grow and blossom.
> One might as well order back the buds
> as to defy the irresistible intention of man
> to be better.[2]

I believe that with all my heart. Deep within us is the hunger for the best and a rebellion against the shoddy and the bad. I have a friend who has rediscovered the Church and its fellowship. He grew up in a good home, but somehow he wandered far from his father's house. He married and divorced, became an alcoholic and lost his job. Then, when he was going down for the third time, he was led back into the Church of his childhood. He writes to me now and again and always he speaks with a kind of wonder at such simple things as worship, prayer, the minister calling, taking his children to Sunday school. All this he thought he had given up and forgotten, but it was always there deep in his life and it represented his real self. A man in Brazil told me that the great lack in that country was our American system of Sunday schools. He meant that when men have memories of this training ground of the Church there is something to draw them back when they would throw off all moral restraint. A good experience is never lost completely.

The ordinary man may act as if he never expects things to get better in his city, his country, or his world. But the very knowledge that things are not right speaks of something he cannot deny or escape. He cannot get away from the vision of something better in the civic life of his community and he cannot quite adjust himself to the idea that there must be no improvement. So a man may try to adjust himself to the presence of evil, but conscience keeps breaking in, and a sense of an indebtedness to the best will haunt him until he dies.

Here is the only safety we have. If we ever lose our confidence in this truth about ourselves, we could not believe in the final victory of goodness. That men should at times move perilously close to a loss of such faith is not to be marveled at, for we have seen evil unparalleled and we have watched civilized people return to savagery. No wonder that the scars made by the dictators do not disappear, nor do the wounds heal even after their death. With infinite patience for those who have gone through sufferings too horrible to describe, we must restore faith in goodness by being good. We believe that goodness has a greater appeal to men that evil. It is the confidence of men who have been captured by Christ that when men see him, they cannot resist him. A man's choice may not always be a good one, but no man is ever satisfied until his choice is right.

There is carved on the base of one of the huge sculptured figures outside the Archives Building in Washington, D.C., this inscription: "The Past is Prologue." That does not mean that the past is meaningless or unimportant. History is not bunk. It means that mankind is uncaptured by the past and its eyes are on the future. It means that the dreamer is an essential part of the race and speaks deep to its heart. It means that the past tells us that our destiny will be determined by what captures us.

When an ideal of right behavior really possesses us completely, it gives us power. Peter Freuchen, who was in Denmark during the war, has told of what happened to the Danish Jews. The Germans announced they would put the same policies into practice there as elsewhere. But the King of Denmark said that his people would never stand for this crime against humanity. He put the yellow arm band on his own sleeve to identify himself with the Jews, and he asked his people to do the same. The Nazi atrocities were not committed in Denmark. They were forbidden by the moral power of a great king and a brave people.[3] There is a sense in which all our moral progress is dependent on this wonderful fact that we are capturable creatures, And, best of all, men are finally to be captured only on the highest levels, for this is the way God has made them.

2. LEGITIMATE IMPORTANCE

For another thing, Jesus Christ gives men the power to become important in a legitimate way. The saint may not crave the same success as the millionaire, but he has his purposes which he serves with all his might. We are speaking of something with very wide implications and ramifications, but we are also speaking of something well-nigh universal.

Now, this desire to be someone important often leads people into dark realms. Children sometimes illustrate this tendency, especially in modern times when discipline has been minimized and free expression has been emphasized. On my way home from Honolulu I was sitting on the sun deck of the *Lurline* and talking with two bishops of the Methodist Church. Our eight-year-old niece was with us on the trip and she had found few companions aboard, since most children were in school. She sat beside me for as long as she could stand it, and then broke in brightly: "Would you like to hear a riddle?" Now frankly, that was the last thing I wanted to hear just then, for we were talking about a most interesting situation in the Church. Besides I had heard the kind of riddles she had picked up from her friends. But it came to me suddenly that here was a little girl who felt neglected and she was saying to me, "I'm here too. Let me into this circle. Do not ignore me. I'm important."

Criminologists tell us that the craving for importance is one of the drives toward crime. Young people who have failed to achieve anything noteworthy in their homes or in their schools turn to a lawless life as a means of getting into the headlines. Crime is often the path of least resistance for people who lack the character to follow the way of hard work. Yet it is no doubt true that some youngsters, having been denied their rightful encouragement, choose crime over anonymity.

Hollywood symbolizes this craving for recognition by movie people. There was a time when a scandal in the life of an actor or actress was a serious matter and often meant the end of a career. But no longer! We can see the general lowering of our moral standards by the way we accept the most repulsive, cheap behavior on the part of our public heroes and heroines. Instead of hurting them, it seems to help them, until one draws the conclusion that any kind of publicity, including the bad, is to be desired. An English princess must deny herself the privilege of marrying a divorced man, but the princesses of the American public are under no such restraint.

The path of statesmanship is long and arduous, but there is always the way of the unprincipled politician. He may appeal to the baser instincts of certain groups and symbolize all that is worst in our democracy. His very crudity and vulgarity seem to be assets for a time, for such behavior implies that he is a man of the people. Politicians dare not be known as men who read books, attend college, or have a taste for good music, art, and literature. Are we so impressed with any kind of notoriety that it will gain our support and our votes? Can we no longer see the difference between the worthy and the merely noisy?

There is no class safe from the vulgar desire to gain importance by getting publicity at any price. The ministry has its share of such men and their lives are full of sound, which seems to impress a considerable number of laymen for a considerable length of time. Such ministers never end up very well, but they hold some of the large places for longer than is right. I saw sometime ago that an American minister was advertising himself as one of America's "most respected clergymen." Surely to be respected, even by those who disagree with us, is to be expected as a minimum. This desire to be important can work havoc among even the best of us.

Yet, let us agree that a man is important and ought to have a sense of great personal worth. It is not a Christian teaching that men are to be regarded as mere ciphers. Far from it! We are the ones for whom Christ died, and we have been redeemed at very great sacrifice. The price of our redemption was the Crucifixion, and God Himself acted to make us good. The status of a man is always raised to its highest level in a Christian society. This is the decisive difference between Christianity and the totalitarians. They may put the state before people, but we cannot put anything above the welfare of human beings. Even the man lowest in the social scale has a divine dignity in our eyes, and this we must respect.

Men are important for what they stand for. Our importance lies in the principles we embody. Much can be made of the passing phases of life, and there is a sense in which we are the most frail of creatures. But a man can stand for the eternal value and can represent something that will be here long after he has gone. The principles for which we make sacrifices make us important. Many a man finds greatness in a great cause. The well-known figures of a generation fade away in a short time, but the quieter men of character grow with every passing year and even after they are dead their names are remembered.

During World War II there was a sign over the desk of some of the broadcasters sending messages to enemy countries. It read: "Is what you are saying worth a man's risking his life to hear?" To all of us there comes the question: Is what you are doing important enough to be worthy of one for whom Christ died? One of the greatest gifts of our Lord is a revelation of how cheap some of our ambitions are, and how priceless are the purposes he gives us. To become a part of his fellowship, among many other things, makes us become important.

3. THE VICTORIES OF THE FAITHFUL

In the third place, Jesus Christ makes us become victorious. It is a victory that is hard for us to recognize at times, and it repels us with its high demands. But the Christian who follows Jesus, is sure to find the secret of victorious living.

He gives us victory over ourselves, which is important. It is hard for me to believe that my worst enemy is within me. It is much easier to believe that somewhere outside myself lies the obstacle, either in my circumstances or in my companions. If I could only change this environment, or this condition, or this duty, then it seems to me that all would be well. But the gospel insists that there can be no victory until I conquer myself. That is my toughest battle.

When a man prays, he will not find it difficult to ask for deliverance from his external opponents. He will ask that this group cease blocking his plans or that this rival be confounded in his attempt to grasp what rightly belongs to him. But it takes more grace than most of us can muster to begin by asking for victory over the sin in our own hearts. I can confess for the sins of the whole world, but it is not easy sincerely to confess the sins which are my own. I suppose that the man who has learned that the real victory is over himself has learned the essential truth about himself.

The evil habit that is too strong to overcome is like a cancer in the body. It can hardly be expected to keep its place, and it must either be removed or it will kill. There are some things we cannot learn to live with and the sooner we come to terms with that hard fact the better. We do not today speak often about the power of Christ to break bad habits, but some of us have found in such experience the convincing proof of his power. Many a plain man who could not stand up to even an elementary theological argument knows that he has been set free from a terrible drive that he could not conquer by himself. In that conviction he rests in the assurance that such power is available to him at all times. It transforms his life with triumph.

The victory over the self is also a victory over the world. One of the most quoted and least understood words of Jesus is in the Gospel of John: " 'In the world you have tribulation; but be of good cheer, I have overcome the world' " (16:33). Did he mean to say that one could escape the world? No, for he did not advise his followers to flee from it and he did not himself try to escape it. There is nothing in the Bible nor in Jesus' teachings to suggest that we ought to hate or despise the world. God made it, and one of Christianity's central affirmations is that neither the flesh nor material things are in themselves evil. Christ refused to call on armies of angels to destroy his enemies. What does it mean that in him we can overcome the world?

It means, I think, that in Jesus we see the world in its proper perspective. We do not try to make permanent what is by its nature evanescent. We can appreciate the world with its beauty, but we must not worship it. We shall leave it one day, and it is not the abiding place of our treasures. We see in Jesus that this world is not our home and, though we are earthly creatures, the essential truth about us and the source of our uniqueness lies in our heavenly citizenship. To overcome the world means to sense the ultimate tragedy of human life and to find something beyond that tragedy in God.

In Greek mythology, one man asks of another, "O Iole, how did you know that Hercules was a God?" and Iole answers: "Because I was content the moment my eyes fell on him. When I beheld Theseus, I desired that I might see him offer battle, or at least guide his horses in the chariot race; but Hercules did not wait for a contest; he conquered whether he stood, or walked, or sat, or whatever he did." So it is with Jesus Christ. He is walking the dusty roads of Palestine, but he still conquers. He is mocked and crucified, but he conquers. With him we are content, for we know that in him and in his victory we shall find our peace and our victory.

4.   THE ETERNAL QUALITY

God in Christ also gives our lives an eternal quality. This is the final test of any way of life, for whatever else we may escape, there is no escape from death. We become clever at pretending this is not a vital matter, but just when we think we are safe, Death demands an answer.

Arnold Toynbee, in one of his writings, speaks of the march of saviors. There are so many at the beginning, he says, who will promise salvation, but in the long march of mankind they fall, one by one, by the wayside. First, the swordsmen fail, then the archaists and the futurists, and then the philosophers. At last only the gods remain, but few of them dare to put their claim to the test of death. Finally, there emerges the solitary figure of the Risen Christ. His presence fills the whole horizon.

The doctrine of the Resurrection is something quite different from the belief in immortality. Here we stand in the presence of a mighty act of God as if through the Crucified One a power to become immortal had been bestowed on all men. It was this mighty revelation of power over death that changed history and made an indelible imprint on mankind. In this climax of the greatest story the world ever heard, God bestows His power to become master of fear and sin and death. A recent book by Frank Laubach includes this dedication: "To all who are dissatisfied with what they are doing for the world." The Resurrection is for all who are dissatisfied with what they are in the world.

The human tendency is to make heroes of the brutal and ruthless. Power of any kind has a terrible attraction for all of us. In his day Sir Walter Scott objected strenuously to the glorification of Napoleon. It will not be strange if a cult dedicated to the worship of Hitler arises. But none of this makes men better or improves the world. How different was Jesus, and how wonderful is his ability to touch our human frailty with the light of eternity. We cannot do better than quote those marvelous words of Albert Schweitzer:

He comes to us as one unknown, without a name, as of old by the lakeside he came to those men who knew him not. He speaks to us the same word, "Follow thou me," and sets us to the tasks which he has to fulfill for our time. He commands. And to those who obey, whether they be wise or simple, he will reveal himself in the toils, the conflicts, the suffering which they shall pass through in his fellowship, and as an ineffable mystery, they shall learn in their own experience who he is.[4]

It cannot be put better.

We are in a realm far beyond logic and, indeed, argument seems the most futile of procedures. There is no convincing argument, and at last we are driven back to the invitation: Come and see. But to those who believe on him there comes the assurance that life is more than a few passing years, and men are more than the animals. This quality of life comes to men now, and it is obviously something far more than the promise of endless existence. We have not truly grasped the Christian doctrine until we see that it begins at the very moment when a man says yes to Christ.

The great pioneer of the Chinese Republic was Sun Yat-sen. He was a young revolutionist who, facing impossible odds, still dreamed and worked for a new and democratic China. Often he was lonely and neglected. He came to America to raise funds for his work. The revolutionists left behind became impatient and rose up and overthrew the dynasty representatives in the province of Kiangsi. Sun Yat-sen was declared the first president. He saw the news first in a newspaper he was reading on a train in a western state. He sat there in a dingy day coach alone and unrecognized. As Pearl Buck said, it is fascinating to imagine his thoughts that day as he read the tremendous news.[5]

When Christians receive the good news of eternity from Jesus Christ, they are "heirs of God and fellow heirs with Christ" (Rom. 8:17). They are the children of the King. To every man who responds to his call, and who believes on his name, the Lord bestows the power to become captured by the best, the important, the victorious, and the eternal.

II

To Bring Forth

THESE WORDS ARE FROM HEZEKIAH, KING OF JUDAH, AND WERE spoken to Isaiah the Prophet: "This day is a day of distress, of rebuke, and of disgrace; children have come to the birth, and there is no strength to bring them forth" (2 Kings 19:3). The country was in trouble, due to a revolt that was premature. The vassal states under the control of the Assyrian Empire were always restless and waiting for an opportunity to regain their independence. When such an opportunity seemed to present itself in the eighth century B.C., Hezekiah joined the Babylonian ruler and the Syrian and Palestinian kings in throwing off the yoke. At first everything went well, but in 701 B.C., Sennacherib, the Assyrian emperor, crushed the revolt and moved on Jerusalem.

In spite of the payment of a huge indemnity, the Assyrians approached the gates of Jerusalem and demanded unconditional surrender. They taunted the Jews with their hopeless situation and asked where they could possibly turn for help. It was in this dark and desperate hour that Hezekiah sent his word to Isaiah describing the terror of the situation and the blackness of the outlook. What shall one do now? was his cry.

It is foolish, of course, to pretend that any two periods of history are exactly alike. Once a man gets that idea in his head he can never see the situation clearly, for he tries too hard to establish a pattern. Beware of historians with theories. There are too many details that are new or different. Likenesses can easily be merely superficial and parallels may be more apparent than real.

Yet it is true that we can learn from the past. The human heart does not change very much and the moral law remains the same. From the past we learn something of the future and from previous crises we find light for the present decision. Without pressing the similarities too far, we can say that Hezekiah's description of his time can be applied to ours. If we follow through the points that ancient king made we may find an Isaiah to bring us a word of assurance. There is such a word, if we can find it.

It is not true, of course, that we are in immediate danger of invasion. At least there is no army thundering at our gates and demanding either surrender or destruction. At the moment there is no power which could force itself on us as the Assyrians threatened to invade Judah. Yet there are insidious doctrines which are hard to keep out, and there are ideologies whose acceptance would spell doom for democracy. We have discovered no protection against thoughts and in a world where great powers are fighting for the minds of men, it may not be too much to say that we are surrounded by danger.

I.   A DAY OF DISTRESS

To begin with, Hezekiah said that his was a day of distress, and so is our day. Societies face problems so great that there seems to be no answer and no solution. Let any man face the world situation with honesty, and he will feel that we are against something beyond our power to control. Too much is happening at one time, as if the dams had broken and the whole sea was at flood. We find ourselves fighting on a thousand fronts and trying to stem a thousand backrushes. The very immensity of our world problems makes us shudder.

There comes over us from time to time a nostalgia for simpler days and smaller problems. This homesickness manifests itself in an attempt to cling to outworn clichés, as if the repeating of those comfortable shibboleths would restore the past. Sometimes our retreat takes the form of pretending that all the complicated mess can be dealt with by using a few simple formulas. It soon becomes apparent that the modern world demands much more than a retreat to the past.

There is a kind of sadness about a group of men gathering in a comfortable club and talking as if they still lived in the nineteenth century. As one of my friends put it, you feel in such a group as if you had seen a dinosaur walking down Broadway. But the Communist pressure refuses to ease, and the spreading demand for independence refuses to ebb. We cannot let go of things, and if we cannot see clearly the way ahead, we certainly can find no means of retreat. As was never true of us before, we must maintain a huge military establishment and American boys must keep the watch thousands of miles from the continental boundaries of the United States. Billions must be voted to help people on the other side of the earth. We spent billions to bomb our enemies into submission and then spent billions to restore their economy. If a man has a passion for logic, this is a poor time to live.

A business executive complains that whenever a problem gets to him it is a crisis. That is the way we all feel. Our daily diet is crisis. There are a dozen places where a new war might break out. There are a score of nations who threaten to sell out to the highest bidder. There are a hundred places demanding our action and our help. Just when we think we have taken care of one dangerous situation, another one appears behind us. It is difficult to see that we are making any progress. Worst of all, we appear to be doomed to endure this distress for a long time to come. For as far ahead as we can see there is no respite.

Everything is interdependent and nothing seems to be aloof from anything else. A few bus drivers decide to go on strike and the whole city is tied up. An Israeli border patrol fires on an Arab position, and the whole world trembles lest it be the signal for a Third World War. An industrial nation raises its tariff, and ten thousand miles away families suffer economic disaster. An empty-headed politician makes a speech full of foolish boasting, and communism gains a thousand new supporters. A Negro boy is murdered in America, and the news spreads across Africa like wildfire.

I do not like this situation any more than the next man, for it is frightening to live in the shadow of an avalanche which may be started by some foolish word or deed of mine. We wish that we could make a few mistakes without the world learning about it. We would like to be able to let off steam now and again without jeopardizing our international relations. We feel like the American Indians must have felt when they found themselves helpless to hold back the tide of white settlers. Every year found their boundaries shrinking and their privacy further invaded, and all they wanted was to be left alone to enjoy what they already possessed. A time of distress, indeed!

Because we are all so mixed up in this circumstance, it is hard for us to keep clear the distinction between what we believe and what we hate. The stain of the enemy's philosophy seeps into our thinking and behavior. Seeking some way out, we sometimes appear to be no different than those we fight. This, too, is a part of our distress, for we must fight a ruthless enemy and yet maintain our own integrity.

Too much responsibility has come upon us too suddenly. We have not had two hundred years to learn about the administration of power. We have not grown into this world supremacy gradually, but with something like a sudden plunge into a maelstrom. We cannot easily send our men to fight holding actions or to attack frontiers we have never seen. The burden is too heavy, and we resent carrying for others what we have always been taught each man should carry for himself.

It is no wonder that some men suffer nervous breakdowns and others find it hard to see their way clearly. Here is an inscription which defines our mood: "Our faith is degenerate in these later days. There are signs that the world is speedily coming to an end.

Children no longer obey their parents. Every man wants to write a book. The end of the world is evidently approaching." Of course, it affords us some comfort when we note that these words were found on an old Assyrian tablet which dates to 2800 B.C. Apparently ours is not the first age to resent its burden of distress, but it is doubtful that any previous age had greater provocation.

When the distress becomes too great, many men find refuge in a religious interpretation of the events. A neighbor of mine told me not long ago that it was foolish to pray for peace or to get worked up about atom bombs. All such matters, he said, are in the hands of God and we have no responsibility for them. He went on to quote some Scripture which indicated that the end of the world would soon be here. Why worry? I must confess that there are times when I envy men who can accept such a viewpoint. What a great relief to be freed from personal responsibility and personal concern! Yet it is hard to see how such a retreat is justifiable in the light of the Bible. If there is one great theme that runs through the Book from the beginning to the end, it is personal responsibility. God gives men power, but He does not give them a release from duty.

It may be that this retreat into obscurantist religion is better than cynicism and fear. For the cynic and the coward only hasten the debacle and help to make it inevitable. It may be argued that a negative kind of faith is better than no faith at all, though it is not much better. But the naked cynicism and the indecent fear exhibited in such times are witnesses of what distress does to the unreligious. We are saved from panic only by faith, and faith is the gift of God. It was a good thing for Judah that Hezekiah was the kind of king who turned immediately to Isaiah. For in a day of distress that is the only source of succor.

Days of distress overwhelm us with the sense of disaster and we do not see things in proper perspective unless we are men of faith. A second-year medical student, discovering diseases he had never heard of before, was filled with a deep sense of foreboding. "I used to wonder why anybody ever died," he said. "Now I wonder why anybody lives." So it is with optimists who suddenly find things worse than they expected. The day of distress is difficult for every man, but for the man without faith it is disastrous.

2.   REBUKE AND UNDERSTANDING

In the second place, Hezekiah said to Isaiah that it was a time of rebuke which was a good insight and a most hopeful understanding. The king did not complain that all of this was undeserved and then spend his time bitterly upbraiding the Almighty. He had grace enough to recognize that he was being rebuked for sin. I once saw a gravestone in a Montevideo cemetery inscribed with a long list of complaints against God for taking the life of a loved one. With a kind of pitiful bravado, this person had carved into stone his anger at God. But it did not strike me as a brave defiance, but as merely a childish tantrum. Nobility was not in it, and no dignity. Man is out of his proper role when he defies God. He shows his true greatness when he takes distress as a rebuke.

Hezekiah had ears to hear the sound of chickens coming home to roost, and so should we. In Judah's case, it was an ill-considered revolt that had backfired. In our case, it is a number of things that have finally caught up with us. If we can accept this truth about the present situation, it will contribute much good to us and to the world.

Woe unto us if we fail to see judgment in our time of troubles. It is a judgment on our inability to enter sympathetically into other peoples' points of view. If I am not careful I find myself saying when traveling in another country, "Why don't these people do things the way we do them? Why are they content with inefficiency and delay? How can they, following their path, ever amount to anything?" Yet in my more contemplative moments I wonder if they do not have something to teach me that I need to learn. The Puritan qualities of hard work and frugality have never appealed to some nations and societies. We hear American businessmen complain about the natives who refuse to work like Americans. Well, perhaps they prefer other values which we have missed.

It may be that in this difficult time we shall find it necessary to enter more sympathetically into the ways of other cultures. That will be a good thing for us. It may come as a shock that we cannot order obedience and respect. It may hurt our pride to learn that there is much in the so-called American way that others do not particularly desire or appreciate. There is little doubt that our culture is dominant, but there is also little doubt that this fact does not always create friends. More times than we like to think, it arouses resentment. Perhaps the time is past when we dare to regard a man as stupid if he does not speak English, or seems ill at ease in the rush of an American city. Maybe we must learn that by putting our worst foot forward in the movies we have not won understanding or admiration. Can it be that it takes a day of distress to rebuke us for our ruthlessness and impatience?

This is a day of rebuke for our pride. If we hesitate to eliminate all signs of racial discrimination, an African continent may go communist. That is something we dare not contemplate. It must be prevented at all costs. Yet we are beginning to suspect that it cannot be prevented if we continue to follow some of our racial policies. Has God put us into the dilemma where we must choose between keeping our white superiority or losing our life? Do you suppose there is a kind of bitter humor in a situation that places us on the receiving end, instead of the giving end, in our relations with our brethren of color?

We are being rebuked because we assumed we were supermen when we are only men. The young gods who break the supersonic barrier still get their hearts broken. The scientific genius who can manipulate atomic power still finds it takes loving patience to bring up his children. The man who sits in the big office and directs ten thousand employees still finds it difficult to control his habits. No, we have not been freed from the ordinary human virtues and temptations, and it is in that realm that final success or failure lies.

Alexander the Great is reported to have said that he hated to make love to a woman because it made him feel human. There may be legitimate reasons why a man should not make love to a particular woman, but that reason is not one of them. Perhaps we have been trying to escape our humanity and set ourselves free from the humility of being earthbound creatures. A day of distress brings us back quickly enough to the truth that all our progress is only a thin veneer over a sinful and dependent nature.

One of the greatest things about Israel was her ability to see rebuke in distress. An ordinary people would have been swallowed up by her enemies and overwhelmed by her sufferings. But not this little chosen nation! For she never lacked a leader to interpret her sufferings in terms of judgment, and she felt her troubles were somehow related to God's love. Now and again she was lifted to a height where she could believe that her sufferings were in some way beneficial for the world and that the stripes of the Suffering Servant would bring healing to the nations. Other people might measure their religion by their success, but not Israel. The purifying fire of distress rebuked her sin and disciplined her life.

Families sometimes find trouble the only means of bringing them back together. During the Depression some families found themselves. In their prosperity they had fallen apart and each member had sought his own way. No one cared much about what was happening to the others and the family disintegrated. Then, in the day of financial reverse, it was discovered that they had to form a united front again. It was now a matter of survival and each had to help the others and do his share by bringing his contribution into the common treasury. I have heard people testify how those hard times redeemed and purified their common life.

Failure can destroy us, but it can also drive us to deeper understandings. I do not know anything like disappointment to bring me to a new sympathy with my brethren. I am afraid that if God did not give me setbacks my poor life would swell up and burst with pride. There is always hope for us if we can say that this time of distress is also a day of rebuke.

Lord Dunsany said something about these times that ought not to be forgotten:

There is a great tendency nowadays to place technique above inspiration, and, if the notion spreads, we shall have the diamond cutters valuing their tools more highly than the diamonds, with the result that, as long as they cut them in accordance with the rules of the craft, they will cease to care whether they cut diamonds or glass, and then will cease to know.[2]

Is this the process that has overtaken us and is this time of trouble a revelation of our disease? It may be that our cleverness is developing techniques and our lack of interest in inspiration has caught up with us. We cannot save ourselves or our world by technique alone. Without a faith to share, we are poor and destitute. Silver and gold have value, but it is better to tell a man to stand up and walk. We have become highly skilled in cutting, but some of our vaunted products appear to be suspiciously glasslike.

3.   THE HOUR OF DISGRACE

The time, said Hezekiah, is not only a day of distress and rebuke, but it is also a day of disgrace. Sociologists have been pointing out that a crisis produces, on the one hand, the best and, on the other, the worst. Thus you will see heroism and thievery side by side. You will see deep devotion to duty and a cowardly attempt to salvage everything possible for oneself. The crisis for some will reveal deep wells of nobleness and concern, while for others it will reveal unsuspected selfishness. There is a sense in which the days of distress are revelations of character or lack of it, so that what has been hidden is now revealed.

The day of disgrace or blasphemy is a time when men set up

the idols in the temple. The idea that God ought to provide prosperity has never died out, and when the day is judgment, then some people decide to find other gods. It is as if a kind of madness takes hold of the unstable and drives them to superstition and magic.

Our generation has seen the rising of ancient cults and the rebirth of old gods. It was hard to believe that leaders of civilized, modern, Christian nations could get a following by preaching hatred of Christ and love for Thor. But it has happened. Once again the Abomination of Desolation is set up in the Holy of Holies. In the very time when unity is demanded if we are to survive, the pagan idols of separateness are revered.

A racial theory which is pure madness in our modern world is carried to its final conclusion in South Africa. The time has long since passed when an absolute separateness was workable. Such a society is like a cancer in the modern world, and it threatens the life of all of us. Is there such a thing as an impulse to mass suicide?

In our enlightened land we see the marks of a pagan worship of exclusiveness. We will maintain our superiority even if it means our defeat. Thus we counsel the use of food as a weapon, giving it to those who will do our will and withholding it from the independent and stubborn. We should not marvel if an Indian father does not love America, for while his child starved we debated when and how much surplus wheat we were going to send.

Our danger is that we shall set up our tribal gods again and desert the worship of the Father of all mankind. The need today is for the restoration of faith to men whose terrible experiences have nearly destroyed all faith. In 1950, a book entitled *Documents of Humanity* was published. The material was gathered by some professors at Göttingen University who had been caught up in the horrors of the mass expulsion of East Germans in 1945. Here are simple stories of desperate people who received some unexpected kindness from those who were supposed to be their enemies. It is one of the most moving records I have seen and it cannot fail to touch the heart deeply. Here in the midst of the worst was found the best. But there is so little of this goodness in the center of so much terror.

Perhaps the most disgraceful sight in such a time is the man who will deliberately use the trouble for his own advantage. This is the kind of day when men exploit other men's fears. It is a day that brings the worst to the surface and gives it opportunity that more quiet times would not afford. Old hatreds and old jealousies rise to the top and find a chance to revenge themselves.

The Church has been under fire in a special way. Men who seek to stamp one pattern of thought and behavior on a people fear an institution that is dedicated to the supremacy of conscience and freedom of expression. Modern prophets have been attacked and an effort made to smear their characters with innuendoes and hints of subversiveness. The free pulpits of Protestantism have been criticized, and in some instances all-out attempts have been made to silence them. It has been a hard time for the Church to maintain the right to speak to the conscience of the nation, for many have preferred sweet generalities to prophetic challenge. Hezekiah's word is the right one—it has been a day of disgrace.

The public schools have come under attack even as has the free Church. Teachers have been pressured and badgered and their honored profession has seemed to be one of the least desirable. School boards have tried to forbid the discussion of certain subjects, apparently believing that the best protection for youth is ignorance. Most of our young men will be serving in the military forces of the nation, and many will be abroad in the midst of foreign doctrines and unfriendly critics. Yet in some schools they are not to be taught anything about such systems, nor are they to learn by discussion what the real issues are.

Do we believe that our cause is just and our way right? If so, why should we fear teaching the truth about our enemies and learning the basis of their attack? We have become great by open study of many claims and promises, but we have never tried to protect ourselves or our children from books and ideas. Controversy has been the lifeblood of our progress, and our faith has been in the right decisions of people who are informed. When one observes what happens to a society that stops thinking, experimenting, questioning, one shudders at a blasphemy that prefers minds governed by fear.

Montaigne once wrote: "Man is certainly stark mad; he cannot make a worm and yet he will be making gods by the dozens." This is the basis of our trouble, for we try to make our own gods and fashion them with our pride. In a word, we sink into the sin of idolatry, so that the day of distress and judgment becomes a day of blasphemy. For back of our failure is our preference for the gods of nationalism or race or class or the status quo rather than God. Our only safety is true religion practiced and proclaimed by Christian people.

4. THE GLORIOUS PROMISES

Finally, Hezekiahs word is: "Children have come to the birth, and there is no strength to bring them forth." It is a striking figure. We have not known the literal meaning of that experience, for the mothers of America are not starved beyond power to bring children into the world. But there is a wider meaning for us in this ancient description.

One of the most frightening developments in our time is the way our progress has been captured by war. There was a time when a new scientific discovery thrilled us and we rejoiced in the wider conquest of our environment. Today we are so unsure of the future that these marvelous new advances seem to spell disaster. We assume almost automatically that all these new inventions make our destruction that much nearer and increase the burdens of our survival. Scarcely a word is heard about what such things may mean for our welfare.

Consider medicine, for example. There is talk now about the

possibility of transferring organs from one body to another. What miracles have been wrought already in relation to the heart! When one has traveled in poor countries which lack proper sanitation or diet one comes home and wonders why we lack a message or a program. We seem to have everything and we can teach other people how to gain many of these priceless possessions. When Jesus walked about Palestine, the sick crowded to him because he had the gift of healing. But we have it, too, and we could walk across our world with something of the same glory.

If we ever doubted the importance of the right spiritual environment we can hardly doubt it now. For nothing goes right unless there is an atmosphere of confidence and goodwill. The inventions continue to appear, but they do not change us for the better. There is nothing wrong with our brains, but our hearts are not right. There are so many marvelous things to be brought forth, but there is not the spiritual power to bring them to life. We are an example of how barren and sterile life can become when men invent without spiritual motives. No wonder that men write those terrible books about the mechanical age of the future wherein all that is worth preserving has been lost. For, mark you, mechanical perfection without some striving for Christian perfection ends up in a prison or a hospital.

The responsibility is ours and the failure is at our door. If the Church cannot bring the power of the spirit to bear on our modern achievements, then we shall find that progress is a trap. The ability to bring forth the children of hope and promise is of God. The true measure of our cities is still to be found in the number of good men in them. We can only go forward when we are willing to follow God. It is still true that all we are worth is the good we do and the character we achieve. Greatness comes forth from poverty and destitution, while evil may be the offspring of prosperity and wealth.

Sherwood Eddy, in his autobiography, speaks of his mother's lack of experience with children before he was born. He says that she was an overintellectual schoolteacher who had seldom seen a baby before she looked at him, her firstborn. The family found her weeping uncontrollably the day after his birth, for she had looked at him and was sure he must be an idiot. She was sure the family was keeping this terrible fact from her. Not many babies are impressive when they first arrive, but what they shall become is one of God's miracles. If there is available the spiritual strength to bring them forth into an environment of love and faith, they are the hope of the world.

What we need is what Hezekiah found in Isaiah, namely, a word of assurance. Concerning the enemy at the gate, thus said the Lord: "For I will defend this city to save it, for my own sake and for the sake of my servant David." (2 Kings 19:34).

God is the only source of the power to bring forth all the glorious promises of our civilization. The issues will be determined by Christians who in a day of distress, rebuke, and disgrace, are dedicated to this faith.

To Advance

GOD SPEAKS TO NATIONS THROUGH MEN, AND NO NATION HAS EVER had such adequate spokesmen for the Lord as Israel. In the Book of Deuteronomy, Moses gave the people the word God had commanded. He was interpreting their history for them. After the long years of wandering in the wilderness, the time came for them to turn toward the Promised Land and then to possess it. But the spies reported that the conquest would be extremely difficult, if not altogether impossible. There were strong men to overcome and terrible obstacles to surmount. Then came this direct command: "You have been going about this mountain country long enough; turn northward" (Deut. 2:2-3). The time for a decision had arrived and the long years of preparation were at an end.

There come into the experiences of men and nations those decisive moments when a great risk has to be taken. All that has gone before must now face the testing of the final move. It is no wonder that in such hours men shrink back and counsel further delay. There is so much to lose, and a defeat appears to be much worse than no attempt whatever.

Many an American will remember D day. I was pastor of a midwestern congregation at that time, and we had the sanctuary open from early in the morning until noon. A continuous service of prayer, meditation, and scripture reading was conducted, and many people came for a time and then went on to their daily duties. In the congregation were the ones who had fathers, brothers, sons, and husbands in the mighty attack on the coast of France. After long preparation the decision was made, and the whole enterprise hung in the balance. The Allies had done everything possible to prepare, and at last the command had come: Turn eastward! It was an awful hour, but if the enemy was to be defeated and the promised land of peace won, the decision had to be made.

For every man there are those crucial moments in the significant realms of his life. It may be in his thinking or it may be in his behavior. The smooth development of human life, so dear to the hearts of some educators, exists only on paper. Life is not like that and, while we may object to a crisis theology or psychology which offer no place for nurture and growth, still we grow by choices and decisions. The road comes to abrupt turns and steep grades and we are constantly plagued with unmarked forks. What has our religion to offer us in these trying moments, and where is God when we must decide in a hurry? It is the testimony of the saints that a voice speaks and a vision guides.

I.   THE IMPORTANCE OF THE WILDERNESS

Perhaps we ought to begin by considering the utmost importance of the wilderness experience. The story of the making of a nation out of slaves is one of the most dramatic chapters in history. The achievement of Moses was one of the greatest in mankind's long experience, and quite rightly we regard him as one of the giants. For consider what he began with in the great adventure! Here were slaves, controlled by strong masters, and with no opportunity to prepare gradually for freedom. They had no experience in organizing a judicial system, and they had never learned to choose leaders. Beginning with the most elementary affairs of society and with no previous tutoring, the task was overwhelming. Probably not the least of the problems was the changing of a slave mentality into the attitudes of free men. It is no wonder that it took a generation and that forty years were spent in the wilderness. The marvel is not that it took so long, but that it could be done at all.

Whatever evolution may mean—and certainly it means many

different theories—it suggests the considerable time necessary to create living creatures. And the process of creation is a continuing one. Things are seldom done by fiat and the thoughts of God are long, long thoughts. When we get in a hurry, we are brought back to the time schedule of the universe, for back of every seeming sudden happening there are many years of getting ready. This seems to be God's way.

It is well for a people to be aware of this in their educational system. Although there is nothing wrong in gaining all the speed possible through the most efficient methods, I am critical of some modern educational theories at this point. The old classical education left much to be desired, for it was aimed primarily at a leisure class rather than at men who would have to earn a living. There was too much Greek, Latin, and Hebrew for a boy who would one day direct an engineering concern. One can spend a disproportionate amount of time in ancient documents, "reading the minutes of the previous meeting," as someone has said. Certainly education ought to prepare us for living in the modern world and ought to teach us how to do what society will demand of us.

Yet we can go too far in the direction of activity and neglect overmuch the cultural background of our civilization. We ought to know something about the books which undergird our life and we ought to feel our roots going down deep into the spiritual heritage which our fathers have bequeathed us. For life is more than the body and more than making a living. A world bound by economic interests is a prison. It is necessary for free men to have some knowledge of the faith which undergirds their freedom. The Promised Land never means what it should mean and is never properly understood unless its citizens know about the forty years in the wilderness.

Men soon betray their inadequacy if they lack preparation for their tasks. We know practically nothing about the boyhood and youth of Jesus, but it cannot be doubted that in those years must lie much of the secret of his grandeur. It is noteworthy that the Gospels speak of his being driven into the wilderness for forty days to be tempted of the devil. This may be a symbolical way of comparing his preparation with that of Israel. At any rate, it came immediately after the inspiration of his baptism experience, and it puts into pictorial language the reality of the testing of Jesus. He was put into the kind of family and environment which made him the heir of Israel's religious tradition. Whatever else "the fullness of time" may have meant, it seems to me that it may quite properly refer to the fact that Jesus came after the necessary preparation had been completed.

Or, there is the experience of Paul. After his experience on the road to Damascus, he went into the desert of Arabia, as he tells us in Galatians. We do not know just where he went nor do we know how long he stayed. However this may have been, the Apostle needed to prepare himself by thinking through the meanings of the conversion experience and setting the main direction of his ministry. It seems to me that long before Paul's conversion experience God had been working on him and preparing him for his work.

Abraham Lincoln's boyhood and youth were lived far from the city, where contemplation and meditation was possible. His early manhood was full of disappointment and failure. To be a lonely child teaches some things that are not learned in happier circumstances. I do not think any man who gave real spiritual and moral leadership to his generation escaped the experiences of loneliness and failure as a part of his preparation. God has a way of making men wander in the wilderness until they are ready for His designs.

This demand for patient preparation is not accepted gladly in our day. I have a friend who has a son in college. I once asked him what the young man was going to do after his graduation. The father replied that he did not know for sure, but the boy was ready to start anywhere—just so it was at the top. That is a reflection of the popular spirit and a description of our notorious impatience. We chafe under discipline and we rebel against the program which holds us back from immediate recognition.

The ministry is a good example of the demand for professional preparation. There are some churches which allow short cuts for bright boys and there are some fellowships where almost anything goes if a congregation can be induced to accept any individual as a minister. Once you begin to set up standards you are accused immediately of stifling the Spirit and putting unnecessary legal obstacles in the path of budding prophets. Once in a while we are probably guilty of this but, on the whole, the demand for hard preparation is sound and beneficial. A day when medicine shows no inclination to ease its demands is a poor time for the Church to be content with less preparation.

I have known a few preachers who had it so easy that they were in the large pulpits almost immediately. They hardly ever impressed me with depth and power. It is easy enough to become popular if you have been given certain gifts, but the men who build the Church and serve the congregation are more than popular. It seems to be necessary to wander in the wilderness if a man is to minister competently as a physician of souls. The young preacher who can grasp this truth early is on his way to a ministry that becomes more like a glorious pageant with every passing year.

Other peoples have not become so infected as Americans with this general hurry for a prominent place in the Church. Perhaps we idealize what is merely farther away, but it seems to me that men in small parishes in England do more solid intellectual work than is true with us. At least some of the first-rate volumes have come out of country parishes where a man had more time for study and writing than the city pastor knows. Our tendency is to count the years in the small places as wasted, while we wait impatiently for the Church to recognize our worthiness for the big place. It is too bad, for it robs the Church and it spoils the man.

In 1754 George Washington was in a bad situation. He had been defeated at Fort Necessity, according to his critics because of a refusal to wait for proper reinforcements. He was accused of preferring personal glory to victory. His officers were called drunken debauchees, while his report on the French plans were labeled a scheme to promote the crooked promotion of a land company. No one would have thought this young man in his twenties had much of a future. His biographer Douglas Freeman writes these significant words about the situation: "Just when one is about to exclaim about some mistreatment, 'What an outrage!' one reflects and says instead, 'What a preparation!' "[1]

The wandering in the mountain country is essential. No experience is useless, for in learning the fine art of living everything is grist for the mill. The years which seem so long at the beginning get short enough when we become wise enough to grasp all the things we need to learn. I believe that God has a time schedule for a man's life and for the achievement of any worth-while thing. Let us accept it gracefully, and at last we will be able to give thanks for it.

2.   THE DECISION TO MOVE

However, if we do come to terms with the necessity for preparation, there is yet another problem facing us. It usually comes later in life, though not always. It is the difficulty of deciding to move after the preparation has been completed. Here is the temptation that faced Israel, and Moses' word was a demand that there be no more wandering in the wilderness. The time had arrived to turn northward and embrace the struggle for the Promised Land.

It is true that men sometimes prefer a continual getting ready to the risking of a decision. Preparation can become an end in itself instead of the means for achieving the goal. Chateaubriand spoke of the temptation to agree to easy solutions and thus to put up with a century of bondage rather than endure the fuss of an hour.

It is a common tendency to temporize and to postpone the grappling with an unpleasant situation.

Procrastination is a universal trait and a very common besetting sin. No one says that he is not interested in the Promised Land, nor does he attack the desirability of its possession. We do not state baldly that we prefer vice to virtue, injustice to justice, slavery to freedom. Not at all! We say merely that this is not the time for insisting on virtue, or justice, or freedom. We will wait for a more convenient season, and we will not destroy what has been achieved by hurrying the process just now. And there are always a hundred arguments for such a position.

Take, for example, the writing of a book. Here is a man who is going to write a book. He has it in his mind and, perhaps, he has a title chosen. All he is waiting for is more time, because just now he is too busy; but one day when he has the opportunity, we may expect a book from him.

Whether it is really important that a man should write a book is certainly a debatable question. There is an old legend which says that when the devil was asked the reason for his fall, he replied, "I wanted to be an author." It may be so. But the point is that most of these intentions are never fulfilled, because a man never does have the time. This kind of achievement is possible only for the man who gets up in the morning before other men arise and goes to bed at night after most men have retired. Above all, it is done only by the man who seats himself and begins to write. The majority will never turn toward the chair. They merely continue to talk about waiting for more time.

America today faces the test of desegregation, forced into a decision by the Supreme Court. It wish we could say the decision had been forced by the Church, but we cannot. It is apparent that the process is more difficult for some parts of the nation than for others. Yet even in those places of greatest difficulty one seldom hears a Christian counseling repudiation of the Court's decision. But we hear a good many honest church people urging postponement and arguing that desegregation is being forced too quickly. Their argument is that it ought to come naturally and gradually, if it comes at all.

Let us be clear about one thing, namely, that there are people who do not want to end racial discrimination now or at any time. We have no sure way of determining how strong they are, but they are strong enough to make a loud noise and to cause the champions of racial freedom great embarrassment. You will not change their minds by waiting a few more years. There will never come a time when this decent, democratic, Christian action can be taken without opposition. Therefore, the time is now and, instead of being taken too soon, the action is long overdue. If we must put it on the lowest level, our very survival depends on demonstrating democracy to the colored millions of the world. So with charity for all and understanding for even the most blind and bitter, we must push on and complete what we have been preparing to do for a hundred years.

At the beginning of the Civil War, the North had a much-admired general by the name of McClellan. He was a first-rate military man so far as knowledge of the science of war was concerned. There were few men who could as quickly take a mob of raw recruits and turn them into a well-trained army. But after the training was finished, he would not or could not go further. He was not willing to risk a decision. He was not ready, or the odds were against him, or this particular engagement was not wise. An army was something to train and parade. Finally the President, in order to get a man who would act, had to remove him. It may be that none of McClellan's successors had as many gifts, but they were men who knew that a war could not be ended without risk. In the battle of life action may be more important than genius.

If life is no more than the affair of a dilettante, then a safe existence is the goal, as some men apparently assume. Around the graduate schools there linger those students who have one more course to take or one more semester to put in on special studies. The time never arrives for them to leave the school and plunge into their profession. Such persons are intellectual McClellans, fearful of decisions. You cannot call a man a failure if he is still preparing, but as the years pass by, such persons make very little contribution to society. Their lives lack completion.

Now and again I have a young preacher who wants to go back to seminary and take a few more courses. He has not gotten along too well, and he has the idea that another course in counseling, or the attainment of one more degree, will do the trick. Usually he is misled, for he has to learn his lessons in the actual parish and the classroom is no place to find the solution to his problem. Honest self-analysis will probably do more for such young preachers than another five years in a school of theology.

I have a friend with a fine woodworking shop. At least that is what it is supposed to be, although there is very little woodworking that gets accomplished in it. But he has the equipment, and he owns several hundred dollars' worth of power tools. He enjoys showing them to his friends, and it is a delight to see all the bright, shining tools in their places. But try and borrow one of them! Not a chance. Or try to get a demonstration of how they work. No, they are not to be used, but only to be admired. For when you use them, you get them dull, and they might get scratched.

If it is hard to wander in the wilderness, sometimes it is even harder to leave the wilderness. There is a temptation to remain with the familiar rather than risk defeat or disappointment. Like the Hebrews, men can prefer the safety of Egypt to the risk of freedom. It is important that we stay in the country of our preparation long enough, but it is also important that we do not stay too long.

The income tax people once received an anonymous letter which had a fifty-dollar bill enclosed. The note with it read: "Five years ago I cheated on my income tax and I have not been able to sleep nights. P.S. If I still can't sleep, I'll send you the rest of it." Thus we temporize and procrastinate, hoping in vain to solve our problems by half measures. It will not do. There comes a time when God tells each of us that we have waited long enough. Now we must make the decision to overcome the obstacles and enter the promised land.

3. THE AMERICAN RESPONSIBILITY

The voice of God is speaking to America as it spoke to Israel. We, too, have been wandering long enough in the wilderness and we ought to be turning toward the better land. If we think we have already arrived, then it turns out that, until the whole world is brought along, there is no safety for us. Whether we like it or not, we are the leader and the responsibility cannot be escaped nor can it be put off on others. To us there falls the terrible, yet wonderful, demand of God that we lead men to peace and the abundant life.

We have the tools we thought were necessary for the achievement of a peaceful and prosperous world society. In the past the problem centered in adequate power for the development of the poor countries. One of the reasons for their poverty has been lack of oil, coal, electricity, which are costly items and not easily made available. There did not seem to be much we could do for these undeveloped sections except share as best we could, and there was just not enough to go around. Now this is not true. With the development of atomic energy, the source of power has become practically unlimited. We stand on the threshold of a period when all people can take advantage of these resources.

Another of our problems was communication. Work in unity was difficult when it took six weeks to get a message across the ocean and then six months to receive an answer. But with the development of the radio and the telephone, we can speak to all men quickly and easily. In terms of communication, the whole world is now as small as was a Greek city-state in the days of Plato.

Co-operation between neighbors we have always thought to be achieved naturally, but between strangers to be difficult. Granted that we were naïve, still the point was well taken that until we knew something of one another we were unlikely to create unity. Since the Second World War people, especially Americans, have been traveling. Ships and planes are reserved months before the summer season arrives. Our boys in the military forces have been sent all over the world. I shall not forget a preaching mission for the Air Force, and the men I met who spoke of Burma or Morocco as familiarly as I spoke of a neghboring city. My wife and I boarded a plane in Los Angeles, flew over the Arctic Circle to Europe, and spent a week with our European chaplains. We flew from Frankfort to New York, where I spent a day and a half in church meetings. Then we headed south and for the next six weeks we were visiting Methodist missions and institutions in that huge continent of South America. One can do tremendous things in a short time with the aid of flight, and the future promises even greater speed.

But now that we have the tools for the new world in our hands, there comes our real testing. For we show a tendency to prefer the old political methods and attitudes which worked fairly well in the horse-and-buggy days, but are anachronisms now. We try to maintain the same balance of power, the same worship of sovereignty, the same isolation. Everything except our minds and our visions seems to have changed. We are unable or unwilling to make the decisions which will show the world that we propose to move toward the Promised Land of international law and goodwill.

Carl Van Doren wrote a fine book with this significant title: *The Great Rehearsal*. It was, interestingly enough, a book about the making and ratifying of the American Constitution, and Van Doren pointed out that we had gone through a great testing and should have learned the answers to the modern dilemma. While the present world problem is greater and probably much more difficult, its essential nature is the same as we faced in the eighteenth century. We have been through an experience which ought to have prepared us for the task before us.

Have we learned enough to carry our principles out into wider settings? Can we use power in a new way so that it will save us, and not destroy us? Can we respect the rights of minorities? Can we find a way for small nations to maintain their freedom and their dignity within a framework of law? Can we show the way toward the necessary exercise of authority over decisions affecting the general welfare, while leaving liberty in local communities for the ordering of their own affairs? The problems are overwhelming, but they are not different in kind from the ones our fathers dealt with so successfully.

What men need today is a light shining in the midst of the darkness which will assure them that someone knows the path and the right direction. No people is able to solve all the problems for all the peoples, and this is not necessary for our salvation. It is vital for a nation to indicate that the problems can be met with patience and goodwill. It is necessary that a nation inspire men to believe that, although it may make mistakes, its heart is right. Above all, it must assure the common people that its aim is liberty for all, and justice for everyone.

General Carlos P. Romulo of the Philippines gave a thrilling account of a speech delivered at the Bandung Conference by Prime Minister Sukarno of Indonesia. "Anticolonialism is not new," Sukarno reminded his audience. "It was on another night, also in April—but way back in 1775—that the first voice was raised against colonialism . . . when Paul Revere made his ride." Of course, we know what it means to revolt and risk everything for freedom. If there is a nation prepared to live in a time when the world wants no more colonialism and no more discrimination, that nation is our own. When we assume the role of an enemy of all the people who are asking for independence, we reverse our tradition. "America," God is saying, "this is your hour and for this crucial time were you created!"

4. THE TIME IS AT HAND

To each man individually God speaks this word of command many times. He tells us that we have wandered long enough and now is the time to turn toward that land wherein He wants us to dwell. Perhaps no other word is so important for us to heed, for we can temporize and compromise with personal evil for years, and put off indefinitely the decisions which would set us on the road to the good life.

Take habits, for instance. Most of us are trying to live with habits which are wrong. We have apologized for them because others are living with them and still others defend them. But somehow for us they are wrong. There may have been times when we tried to rid ourselves of them, but we failed. We do not want that embarrassment again, and so we decide to accept them. But when it is necessary for us to pray, immediately a habit looms up like a black specter, and our prayers are silenced. Or when we would turn to God in a deeper dedication of ourselves, a habit stands like a wall between us. To all of us in such a predicament, God says: "You have waited long enough. Try once more! Break loose from this imprisonment and become a free man." And, best of all, He promises to help us.

Or it may be a matter of personal relations. Deep in our hearts there is a bitterness, a hatred, a desire for revenge. It spreads through our lives like poison. Perhaps within our family relationships this wrong exists and must be dealt with now. Perhaps in our business life we hate some man above or below us. There is a life of forgiveness and love toward which we ought to be turning, and it cannot be postponed longer.

The Church is full of people who have been hearing about the spiritual life all their days, but they have never actually experienced it for themselves. They pray only spasmodically; they think of God only occasionally; they feel a great emptiness and questioning where they wish there was assurance. To such as these God says that it is time to taste and see that the Lord is good. It is time to enter into the inheritance of the Almighty. Spiritual experience leaves a man not on a cloud, but with his knees strengthened and his head high. It gives him courage, for he learns of resources that are adequate and plentiful. Men cannot live without spiritual experience, and the time to take this seriously is now.

I was preaching in a series of meetings in an eastern city some time ago and the man who directed the singing taught us an old chorus. Here are the words:

> Draw nigh to God
> And He'll draw nigh to you.
> What'er He promises
> That will He do.
> Though an old story,
> It's always been true;
> Draw nigh to God
> And He'll draw nigh to you.

Not great poetry and not great music perhaps, but a phrasing of one of man's greatest experiences. Yours is the decisive move, for you must turn north. In that direction lies the land of freedom, and toward it God directs us. As we draw near it, we discover we draw near to Him.

Notes

1. THE MYTH OF SUPERMAN

[1] Pearson, *Dizzy*, Harper, 1951.
[2] Shaw, *Sixteen Self Sketches*, Dodd, Mead, 1949.

2. THE DELUSION OF POWER

[1] Wallis, *Stories on Stone*, Oxford, 1954.
[2] Garrison, *The Preacher and His Audience*, Revell, 1954.
[3] P. A. Sorokin, *The Ways and Powers of Love*, Beacon, 1954.
[4] William Ernest Hocking, *What Man Can Make of Man*, Harper, 1942.

3. THE MASS MIND

[1] Hyde, *Dig or Die, Brother Hyde*, Harper, 1954.
[2] Doniger, *Religion and Human Behaviour*, Association, 1954.
[3] Heard, *Gabriel and the Creatures*, Harper, 1952.
[4] Quoted by Commager in *Freedom, Loyalty, Dissent*, Oxford, 1954.
[5] Elliott-Binns, *The Early Evangelicals*, Seabury, 1953.
[6] *Harper's Magazine*, July, 1955.
[7] McAfee and Parker, *Near to the Heart of God*, Bobbs-Merrill, 1954.
[8] Religious News Service, Dec. 8, 1952.
[9] Bainton, *Here I Stand*, Abingdon, 1951.

4. PILGRIMS

[1] Sullivan, *Under Orders*, Smith, 1944.

5. PRIESTS

[1] Miller, *The Renewal of Man*, Doubleday, 1955.

6. PROPHETS

[1] Rebecca West, *The Meaning of Treason*, Viking, 1947.
[2] Wieman, *Methods of Private Religious Living*, Macmillan, 1929.
[3] Korngold, *Two Friends of Man*, Little, Brown, 1950.

7. PIONEERS

[1] Wallis, *Stories on Stone*.
[2] Bowles, *Ambassador's Report*, Harper, 1954.

[3] Hallam Tennyson, *India's Walking Saint: Vinoba Bhave*, Doubleday, 1955.
[4] Nathaniel Micklem, *Ultimate Questions*, Abingdon, 1955.

8. PASTORS

[1] Redhead, *Learning To Have Faith,* Abingdon, 1955.
[2] Wilkinson, *Walking in the Light*, Abingdon, 1954.
[3] Robinson, *The Mind in the Making*, Harper, 1921.
[4] Johnson, *The Imprisoned Splendor,* Harper, 1953.

9. PERFECTIONISTS

[1] H. R. L. Sheppard, *Impatience of a Parson*, Hodder & Stoughton, 1927.
[2] Whittaker Chambers, *Witness*, Random House, 1952.
[3] Overstreet, *Understanding Fear*, Harper, 1951.
[4] Meek, *The Life to Live*, Oxford, 1955.

10. TO BECOME

[1] Quoted in Brooks, *Opinions of Oliver Allston*, Dutton, 1941.
[2] Kraft, "The Irresistible Intention," *Christian Century,* Jan. 19, 1955.
[3] Hecht, *A Child of the Century,* Simon and Schuster, 1954.
[4] Schweitzer, *The Quest for the Historical Jesus*, Macmillan, 1948.
[5] Buck, *My Several Worlds*, Day, 1954.

11. TO BRING FORTH

[1] Luccock, *Marching Off the Map*, Harper, 1952.
[2] Fitzgerald, "Literature by the Slide Rule," *Saturday Review,* Feb. 14, 1953.

12. TO ADVANCE

[1] Fosdick, *What Is Vital in Religion*, Harper, 1955.

Index

Set in Linotype Granjon
Format by James T. Parker
Manufactured by The Haddon Craftsmen, Inc.
Published by HARPER & BROTHERS, New York